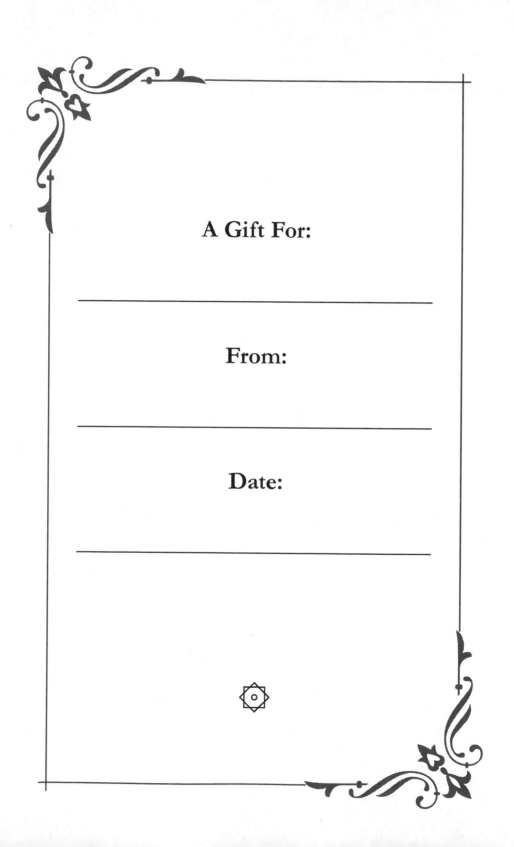

A Gift For:

_____

From:

_____

Date:

_____

MOUNTAINS
OF
GRACE
LIFTING AS WE CLIMB

THE WOMEN OF GRACE WRITERS
AND CONTRIBUTING AUTHORS

WESTBOW
PRESS®
A DIVISION OF THOMAS NELSON
& ZONDERVAN

Scripture taken from the Amplified Bible, copyright © 1954, 1958, 1962, 1964,
1965, 1987 by The Lockman Foundation. Used by permission.

Scripture taken from the Holy Bible: International Standard Version® Release 2.0. Copyright ©
1996-2012 by the ISV Foundation. ALL RIGHTS RESERVED INTERNATIONALLY.

Scripture taken from the King James Version of the Bible.

Scripture quotations taken from the New American Standard Bible®,
Copyright © 1960, 1962, 1963, 1968, 1971, 1972, 1973, 1975, 1977, 1995 by The
Lockman Foundation. Used by permission. (www.Lockman.org)

Scripture taken from the Holy Bible, NEW INTERNATIONAL VERSION®. Copyright ©
1973, 1978, 1984, 2011 by Biblica, Inc. All rights reserved worldwide. Used by permission. NEW
INTERNATIONAL VERSION® and NIV® are registered trademarks of Biblica, Inc. Use of either
trademark for the offering of goods or services requires the prior written consent of Biblica US, Inc.

Scripture taken from the New King James Version. Copyright © 1979, 1980,
1982 by Thomas Nelson, Inc. Used by permission. All rights reserved.

Scripture quotations taken from the Holy Bible, New Living Translation, Copyright © 1996, 2004.
Used by permission of Tyndale House Publishers, Inc., Wheaton, Illinois 60189. All rights reserved.

All Scripture quotations in this publications are from The Message. Copyright © by Eugene H. Peterson
1993, 1994, 1995, 1996, 2000, 2001, 2002. Used by permission of NavPress Publishing Group.

This book is a work of non-fiction. Unless otherwise noted, the author and the publisher
make no explicit guarantees as to the accuracy of the information contained in this book and
in some cases, names of people and places have been altered to protect their privacy.

WestBow Press books may be ordered through booksellers or by contacting:

WestBow Press
A Division of Thomas Nelson & Zondervan
1663 Liberty Drive
Bloomington, IN 47403
www.westbowpress.com
1 (866) 928-1240

Because of the dynamic nature of the Internet, any web addresses or links contained in
this book may have changed since publication and may no longer be valid. The views
expressed in this work are solely those of the author and do not necessarily reflect the views
of the publisher, and the publisher hereby disclaims any responsibility for them.

Any people depicted in stock imagery provided by Thinkstock are models,
and such images are being used for illustrative purposes only.
Certain stock imagery © Thinkstock.

ISBN: 978-1-5127-4660-0 (sc)
ISBN: 978-1-5127-4662-4 (hc)
ISBN: 978-1-5127-4661-7 (e)

Library of Congress Control Number: 2016910104

Print information available on the last page.

WestBow Press rev. date: 07/27/2016

DEDICATION

PORTRAIT OF GRACE

Paula Maldonado

This book is dedicated to Paula Maldonado — wife, mother, grandmother, friend, former Boy Scout leader, counselor and radio disc jockey. Despite numerous surgeries, illnesses, chronic pain, and family tragedies, Paula has remained an inspiration to many with her witty humor, upbeat attitude, loving kindness and gentleness, and especially her steadfast faith and trust in our heavenly Father. In the face of many of life's challenges she is truly a portrait of grace.

CONTENTS

Section 1: AMAZING GRACE
"Be still and know that I am God:
I will be exalted among the heathen, I will be exalted in the earth."
(Psalm 46:10 KJV)

Section 2: THE THRONE OF GRACE

"Let us then approach God's throne of grace with confidence,
so that we may receive mercy and find grace
to help us in our time of need."
(Hebrews 4:16 NIV)

Section 3: SUFFICIENT GRACE

"And he said unto me, My grace is sufficient for thee:
for my strength is made perfect in weakness..."
(2 Corinthians 12:9 KJV)

Section 4: ABOUNDING GRACE

"He waters the mountains from His upper rooms;
the earth is satisfied and abounds with the fruit of His works."
(Psalm 104:13 AMP)

PREFACE

In honor of our mentor and facilitator, author Anita Chadwick Beno[1], we asked her to share words of wisdom to enhance our writings in this book. Her following submission on "Humble Beginnings" is truly just that - humbling, yet it attests to the power of God through ordinary people who commit their lives and means to His will.
That's who we want to be!

"In writing this little piece for your book, my intent was to keep it short and keep the focus where it belongs. The book is not about me. The original group was never about me. I was just the vehicle that guided the group along its journey toward self-discovery. I'm honored that you thought of me again.

FROM HUMBLE BEGINNINGS –
LIFTING AS WE CLIMB

It was a lovely afternoon and my intentions were to go to a meeting of the local chapter of the Daughters of the American Revolution (DAR) in Sierra Vista, Arizona, and meet other ladies and discuss genealogy. Little did I know what God had in store for me!

As I sat in the living room of a very lovely home, my eyes were drawn to a quiet corner of the room. There, sitting by herself, was a beacon of light...Something compelled me to want to get to know her. Finding her was easy. It was like being in a very dark forest and having my flashlight zoom in on her! "Wow," I thought. "I really want to talk to her!" I walked over and introduced myself. And so it began...

She and I became acquainted and she told me that her dream was to start a writing club someday. I said, "Oh, that's really interesting. I love writing too. I'm a retired high school English teacher. I taught creative writing!" "REALLY?" she quipped with a cute little gleam and flicker in her eye. "HUMM." That was the very modest beginning of what was

---

[1] Author of "That April Day: *A Story of Love's Triumph Over the Civil War.*"

soon to become the *Women of Grace Writers*. At first our writing exercises were very basic, but I knew that I was witnessing the commencement of something very special. Sometimes the most humble beginnings lead to the most inspiring and amazing results.

Over 2,000 years ago, something very astonishing began - something that changed the world forever. Christ was born in the most humble way possible. Naked and alone, he needed love and support. We're no different. We all had that same humble beginning. Like Christ, we were naked and alone, and we looked to others for love and support. We had that need to be lifted up, guided, and nurtured. It's when we receive that guidance and Christian love, that we can soar like the great birds of the sky and be strong and confident in what we cherish and in what we believe. And we can share that strength with others and help them on their journey just like the apostles did, for that's what the word "apostle" really means.

As we grow and traverse through life, we sometimes tend to think that we are independent, but in reality we are not. We never lose that need to be loved, guided, and lifted up as we climb upward in our spiritual maturity. We *CAN* be like Andrew, the first apostle, and offer support and encouragement to others while we speak, write, share, and live our own truth. With that love and support of others and our own strength of character, we can make that journey and find our home with our Heavenly Father.

May God bless you and your families. I love you and am richer for having known you. Anita Chadwick Beno June 23, 2015"

ACKNOWEDGEMENT

Special recognition is extended to Rick Whipple, Graphics Design instructor, Cochise College, Sierra Vista, Arizona. His enthusiasm and untiring patience and professional assistance have ensured a quality format and design of the book cover, graphic images, as well as the manuscript. Without his help we could not have achieved all our publishing requirements and writing goals. GOD's grace is always so unique, so timely, and eternally so Amazing.

The LORD's Obedient Servant

"The Sovereign LORD has given me his words of wisdom,
so that I know how to comfort the weary.
Morning by morning he wakens me
and opens my understanding to his will.

The Sovereign LORD has spoken to me,
and I have listened..."
(Isaiah 50:4-5 NLT)

To our readers: "This is our testimony – The Message of our work"
The Women of Grace Writers - 2016

~ Section 1 ~
AMAZING GRACE

"Be still and know that I am God:
I will be exalted among the heathen, I will be exalted in the earth."

(Psalm 46:10 KJV)

A Mother's Love

"And he took the children in His arms, put his hands
on them and blessed them." (Mark 10:16 NIV)

A mother's love! It's so amazing and awesome to watch our female dog nurture, even caress, her puppies. She ever so gently lays her head on each one as if to hug them, with her front paws embracing them. She diligently grooms their every need, keeping them meticulously clean.

As I watch in amazement, I marvel at how fast she reacts to any strange sound that brings her to acute attention. Her protective instinct is always on guard when guests arrive to share in our delight of how God created the animal kingdom. She has such a strong instinct to take loving care of her babies.

It always grieves me when I see or hear about a human mother ignoring or mistreating her babies. God did not create us in His image to be cruel or uncaring. I'm just thankful to be so blessed as I observed Dinky with her tender-loving care and, yes, the necessary discipline also. I count it a privilege.

God in turn created us to love, care, and nurture our children. Unfortunately there are those who abuse their children physically, mentally, and emotionally, and these children often-times become like their parents; the cycle is ongoing. Our world would be a better place if children were raised as gently as some animals care for their babies. God created us in His image to love and care for our children as he created us to do.

"Thank you God for loving us—for nurturing us and reaching out to us in a tender-loving way. Keep your arms of protection around us as animals do to their young."

—Lynne Brown

Away

"Come unto me all ye that labour and are heavy laden and I
will give you rest…I am meek and lowly in heart: and ye shall
find rest unto your souls." (Matthew 11: 28–29 KJV)

"**Away** is a place that can be as far as the horizon - Or as
close as this afternoon" —"**Away** is a place that's easy to
find - And a feeling that's impossible to forget." [2]

These two statements are among several used as "Go RVing" advertising
slogans in various magazines and television spots. Many people here
in Arizona are familiar with the joy of being able to "get away" in a
recreation vehicle (RV). These statements particularly reminded me
that even with only two of us retirees in our house, I still can find
it difficult to *get away*. Maybe just to get away to a quiet retreat center
with your Bible or with a good book and some writing paper—or to
a peaceful place on a park bench, or kicking sand at the shore while
listening to the gulls fly over. That place where you can regroup and
calm your mind from the busy activities of a generally normal lifestyle.

It would be wonderful if we could all enjoy the benefit of a restful
RV vacation or adventure, but God tells us, especially in the passage of
Scripture shown above, that we all can have such a getaway whenever
we need it. We can experience total peace at any time and rest on any
given day, because He says, "Come unto me all ye that labour and are
heavy laden" (v. 28).

Another important aspect of such a getaway is that He also says "I
am meek and lowly in heart" (v. 29)—that is, He lets us know that He
is very approachable and willing to listen to our prayers and to give us
rest for our needy souls. Accordingly, and similar in context as the RV
advertisements, "God is always easy to find and will leave you with a
feeling that's impossible to forget."

—Phyllis Andrews

---

[2] "Campfire Print Ad." Go RVing.http://gorving.com/discover-rving/
our-commercials/campfire-print-ad

Balloons

"Now that you have purified yourselves by obeying the truth so you have sincere love for each other, love one another deeply, from the heart." (1 Peter 1:22 NIV)

My stepfather, John, and I did not always see eye to eye. However, he was very good to my mother and all of the family. I think he was afraid I would come in and take over their lives.

As time went by mother grew frailer, so I arranged my work schedule to be available when needed. As it turned out, she was not the one who really needed me. It was my stepfather. He suddenly became blind from a tumor. It was difficult because he thought he could see—a condition caused by hallucinations. He refused to accept where he was and his being blind. We argued at times because he did not believe me when I explained his condition to him.

Before Mother's death, I promised her I would take care of John as long as I could. But when she finally passed away, he seemed unaware she was gone. Then, less than two months after her death, he also passed.

On the first year anniversary of their deaths, my family and I went to the park to release balloons with messages of love into the sky. Our mother's balloons went up into the sky until we could no longer see them. But a strange thing happened when we released the balloons we had brought for John.

When his balloons went up they tangled together. I possibly was the only one watching as his balloons formed into a heart before they also flew up and away. It seemed to be such a special message of love to me from God. It made all the struggles worthwhile.

—Sue Walker

Blazing Furnace

"Shadrach, Meshach and Abednego replied to him, 'King
Nebuchadnezzar, we do not need to defend ourselves before
you in this matter. If we are thrown into the blazing furnace,
the God we serve is able to deliver us from it, and he will
deliver us from Your Majesty's hand.'" (Daniel 3:16–17 NIV)

"I'm having cataract surgery," a nursing home resident explained,
her eyes reflecting fear. The ministry team immediately prayed with
her and provided encouragement but nothing seemed to relieve her
distress— her "blazing furnace."

Watching the team pray, memories of my experience with major
surgery for cancer came rushing back. Although many years have
passed, I momentarily felt the fear that once held me captive. I recalled
praying for healing to avoid the operating room and all related treatment.
Because of many delays in scheduling, I was certain that God would
heal me without medical intervention; however, to my surprise, God
had another plan.

As the dreaded day approached, my prayers changed from "Father,
heal me," to "Father, if you aren't going to heal me then help me with
my fear of pain and surgery." I wasn't only afraid—I was a coward,
not realizing that my problem was really a lack of faith in my heavenly
Father to do what was best.

Upon arrival at the hospital, I was hastily prepared and placed in
queue for an operating room. Quietly praying as I waited my turn, the
anesthesiologist mistook my demeanor for fear or nervousness. As
he gently spoke with me, I realized I was no longer afraid. God had
answered my prayer. The anesthetic drip started, causing me to drift off
to sleep. Upon waking, I was placed in my room where I noticed that
the pain was tolerable. At one point after surgery, the nurses thought
I was not self-administering enough pain medicine. But, the truth
was—I didn't need so much of it.

After release from the hospital, there were several subsequent visits to the operating room for surgical revisions. However, I never again felt that awful suffocating fear nor did I have unbearable pain—my own "blazing furnace." I experienced the entire ordeal without fear and anxiety, and, as a big plus, with not much pain. I experienced a gentle peace of knowing that Jesus was taking care of me. As a result, my faith and trust in God grew tremendously. Could that have been God's plan all along?

I now realize that God often delivers us through the fire—but not from the fire. Like the Hebrew youths in the book of Daniel, God could have saved them from the "blazing furnace." But instead, He chose to join them in the furnace and rescued them unharmed without even the scent of smoke or singed clothing.

Was this a testimony to the unbelievers? Were the three young men afraid? Yes, I believe they were fearful, but their trust and faith in God was stronger than their fears. And a testimony—King Nebuchadnezzar did not believe that their God would be able to rescue them until he saw the three young men with his own eyes in the "blazing furnace" with a fourth man like "the Son of God." And then they stepped out of the furnace totally unscathed.

Fear is natural in our lives, but becoming a prisoner to it is not. Paralyzing fear is evidence that our trust in God is not where it should be. Fully trusting our heavenly Father, who loves us, is key to conquering our fears and anxieties.

—Juanita Adamson

Butterflies

"The LORD himself goes before you and will be with you;
he will never leave you nor forsake you. Do not be afraid;
do not be discouraged." (Deuteronomy 31:8 NIV)

Butterflies, butterflies—everywhere! But not flitting around like you would expect. It was late August in Upper Huachuca Canyon, Arizona. Butterflies were sitting on the roadway flapping their wings. Only a few flew away as I walked around them. Then, I noticed that more were taking flight. Puzzled at what was happening, I noted some others were resting on the warm damp ground nearby. It seemed odd. But I don't know much about butterflies, except my own casual observation of their beauty and activities as they flit from one flower to another. After watching them for some time, we decided to go home.

Perplexed, I searched the Internet and discovered that when butterflies leave the chrysalis they flap their wings to get the bodily fluids flowing and to dry their scales. They cannot fly until those delicate wings are filled with fluid and the warmth of the day has dried the scales. The weather must reach a certain temperature before they can actually take flight. They stand on damp soil, taking in the minerals they need to survive and to reproduce. As I read the information, I was amazed with the greatness and awesomeness of our Creator and His attention to every detail of a creature that lives only a brief time. I felt privileged to have had the opportunity to observe the careful attentiveness and care our heavenly Father has for the butterfly.

I reflected on times when I wondered whether God was concerned with me and the situations plaguing my being—the minutiae causing me apprehension and unrest. Did God really have time to be aware, let alone to be concerned with my insignificant problems? Did God really see my predicaments or was I just an insignificant piece in the puzzle of life?

As I meditated on the miracle of the butterfly, I realized God's unfailing faithfulness to all of us is just that—constant and unshakable.

Even in the darkest, most chaotic times, God is there, not only guiding but comforting and reassuring us.

God has promised that He is always with us and we are guaranteed that He does not default on His promises. The Bible tells us not to be afraid or discouraged. If God meticulously takes care of the butterfly, how much more concern and care does He have for us?

—Juanita Adamson

Daddy's Message

"Whoever dwells in the shelter of the Most High will rest
in the shadow of the Almighty." (Psalms 91:1 NIV)

I know my mother believed and had faith in God, but my father never said much about it except when I wanted to accept Jesus Christ as my Savior. He wanted me to wait for him so that we could walk down the aisle of the church to the altar together to indicate our decision. That did not happen and, as far as I know, he never publically accepted Christ.

When my dad was passing away it was a struggle. It was hard for him to let go. Even my mother worried about his faith. However, I believe that God shows us signs to bring comfort in our times of need. One night Mother had a dream in which she said that my father "came to her." They stood together and he had his arm around her shoulder. It was something he did often in life. She described the scene as a peaceful and beautiful place. There was a river with a bridge across it. They both stood on one side. He told her everything was okay, then— as she turned to look at him—he was gone. He was across the bridge on the other side.

When Mother awakened from the dream, she felt it was God's way of letting her know that everything was alright. It brought her so much peace.

—Sue Walker

David and Goliath

"From the end of the earth will I cry unto thee,
when my heart is overwhelmed: lead me to the rock
that is higher than I." (Psalm 61:2 KJV)

At one point in my Government career I was just about overwhelmed in my attempt to comprehend an especially difficult point of tax law. I was away from home and living out of a suitcase for weeks during this comprehensive training session. Accordingly, I can empathize with the writer of this psalm who was also going through a "wilderness" experience in his life. David, the proposed writer of this portion of Scripture, was exiled from his home and away from things that were familiar, but he earnestly sought the Lord in prayer. This psalm illustrates the power of prayer when we are in trouble and/or going through uncertain and seemingly insurmountable challenges. The psalmist prays "lead me to the rock that is higher than I."

The night before the critical final exam for my class I was also praying a similar prayer—"Lord, I can't do this without You. I need your help." As I knelt beside the bed in my hotel room I could identify with the fear the Israelites must have felt as David confronted their enemy—that giant Philistine, Goliath. However, as my David-courage kicked in I would then pray my confidence in God and His power to "bring all things to my remembrance," which I had studied during those many weeks before. I further reminded Him—not that He needed a reminder—that this was a huge challenge for me, because I had a personal commitment to not only finish well, but also to succeed in a male dominated position. So, as with the psalmist, I committed my cause to God who promises to hear our prayers. In His omnipotent grace He stretched out His hand and caused peace and pleasant sleep to sweep over my soul that night and ultimate success with the exam that next day. "GOD always specializes in things that seem impossible."

—Phyllis Andrews

Derailed

"See to it that no one falls short of the grace of God
and that no bitter root grows up to cause trouble
and defile many." (Hebrews 12:15 NIV)

Sometimes I liken keeping to the straight and narrow way of God as a railway track! The train represents the church anchored to the railway tracks representing Christ. I am an individual car. Last week my carriage jumped the tracks. I was derailed. I am ashamed to say that it took me two days of introspection and prayer before I realized that I had not only jumped the tracks, but careened off—bumping and jolting wildly through the landscape of my own circumstances. I even had to resort to reading one of my own devotions again, entitled "Ride Through It."

The incident started casually enough. I had made a normal request to my spouse asking for use of our Ford truck in order that I might pull four horses to a three-day camping trip. He gave me a hard time, stating that he needed it. Since we own two trucks, one of which is not well suited to horse pulling, it was not clear to me why he took this position, other than to be difficult. I informed him bluntly and angrily that this was selfish. I asked him what else he would call it. That was the end of the dialog—cold silence followed. My husband had been invited to go on the trip also, but had elected previously not to go due to his school commitments.

Both of us are Christians, but both of us were so irritated with each other that we did not follow God's word and resolve our differences before we went to bed—did not have our usual evening prayer together—and even went so far as to sleep separately. The morning was no better. We neither greeted each other nor said our usual goodbye with a kiss upon leaving the house. I remained hurt and very angry.

I went to the health club and spent two hours, rather than the normal hour, exercising off my frustrations and wondering how I was going to tell my friends that I could not use the truck to pull the horses.

The day continued. I talked to God, but a little voice (Satan) kept intruding—reverberating in my head and validating my opinion of "how selfish my spouse is." With time, I began to calm down. I began, instead of judging my spouse, to look at why he might have taken this position. Nothing specific surfaced, but I did discern that the mere use of the truck was not the real issue.

Finally, the underlying issue did surface, although not directly. I pounced on it like a cat on a proverbial mouse! He did not want me to go on the trip because there were two men and two women, notwithstanding that the two women (me and a friend) would sleep in a separate RV. I respected his point of view, although I wish he had said this upfront, rather than after twenty-four hours of grief between the two of us. I cancelled my trip immediately. With the benefit of hindsight I should have been more sensitive to the core issue.

I am ashamed to admit that only after several days have passed do I now realize how badly I dealt with this entire situation. We cannot change others, but we can look at ourselves and strive for positive change in the future. God's Word provides the instructions.

- First, I should have been slow to anger—I was not.
- Second, I should have been slow to speak—I was not and immediately came to a conclusion that turned out to be incorrect.
- Third, I should have probed gently, given my husband the benefit of the doubt, and attempted to discern what might really be going on. I did not.
- Fourth, I should have taken a hard look in the mirror at how I was behaving.
- Fifth, I should have taken the high road, swallowed my pride, and made forgiveness and reconciliation essential—as the Word says 'do not let the sun go down on your anger'"— I did not.

Oh, how many things I messed up! Sometimes knowing what you should do is blown away in the emotional heat of the moment. I have learned a lesson. I pray for strength that in the future when those hot spirited discussions come—as they certainly will—I can maintain grace and dignity and follow God's instructions and not instantaneously flip, or "jump the tracks," into my own misguided and critical patterns of behavior.

Do you ever get derailed? Do you rerun well-worn negative patterns of behavior? Give them to God and ask for strength to crucify them!

—Catherine Ricks Urbalejo

Follow Me

"Come follow me and I will send you out to
fish for people." (Matthew 4:19 NIV)

The first recollection of my knowledge of God and Jesus was through Little Golden Books.

Before I was able to read I liked to look at the pictures as my mother would read. My brother and I went to church most Sundays. We went to Sunday school, the regular church service, sang in the children's choir and attended Wednesday night services. God "held my hand" all through my childhood years. When I was twelve I felt that He *"called"* me every Sunday as we sang the last song: the song to surrender our hearts to God. I resisted. The call became louder. The louder it became the further back in the church sanctuary I sat. I am, generally, an up-front kind of a person. I told my daddy about wanting to accept Jesus Christ as my Savior (to be "saved").

As he was in the army and stationed away from us he asked me to wait until he got home, when we could walk down the aisle of the church to make that decision together. I agreed to wait. However, God would have none of that. He wanted me now. I had to grip the back of the pew so hard to wait. I would actually be in tears by the end of the service from the struggle to wait for my dad. Finally, there came the day when I felt that God literally *took me by the hand and pulled me down the aisle*. With tears running down my cheeks I accepted Christ as my Savior. My actions upset Daddy, but I never felt guilty as I believed it was God's will.

He has guided my life and my career, and has brought me to "the love of my life." God has also provided me with a church in which I can learn about Him—and serve Him faithfully. I am following Him.

—Sue Walker

God's Mighty Protection

"But let all who take refuge in you be glad; let them ever sing
for joy. Spread your protection over them that those who
love your name may rejoice in you." (Psalm 5:11 NIV)

Five tiers of highway like the tentacles of an octopus, cars careening at high speed around curves, loops, and exits—you might guess a video game or an action movie. But, that would be incorrect! It is actually the experience of driving in and around Dallas, Texas. Yet, few people seem to be afraid as they make their daily trips to work or other activities. What if one of those tiers of traffic should come crashing down? What a horrible disruption that would make in the lives of many.

On a recent trip—armed with God's mighty protection and a Global Positioning System (GPS)—we traveled through the tangled jungle of right and left exits and turns in search of our destination in Dallas. As we zoomed down the road, I wondered why it is so easy for people to have complete faith in fallible men and their imperfect workmanship, yet find it difficult to trust God. Daily, people travel the complex highway systems of concrete and iron rebar without thinking or doubting the durability and indestructibility of such structures, but many distrust God's intervention and protection in their lives.

As we traveled, we experienced first-hand our dependence on God's protection. We were on one of those "exit on the right and stay on the left" moves following the GPS and highway instructions when a plastic and metal dining chair suddenly appeared in our lane. There was no evasive action, without causing a serious accident, to avoid hitting it—we were surrounded by traffic travelling between fifty and sixty miles per hour and a drainage ditch on our left. At the absolutely right time, God gave my husband clarity of thought to make a split-second decision to hit the chair and suffer the consequences of damages to our vehicle instead of serious injury or perhaps death to all six occupants in our minivan and those in other cars. Each of us cringed, sighing thankful prayers, as the chair went under the wheels. Stopping was not an option. Several miles later, we were finally able to stop and assess the damage, which to our surprise, was minimal.

We rejoiced in God's protection and mercy. He was not only faithful to keep us from injury, but protected our property from extensive damage. The minor loss was later repaired free of charge.

Only God could have orchestrated protection for us in this instance. We must trust God to spread His protection over all of us in every circumstance of life.

—Juanita Adamson

I Know

"Be still, and know that I am God." (Psalm 46:10 KJV)

I had the "praying without ceasing" down pat. Daily I dropped to my knees with my list of requests, which always had "my" specific outcomes and timelines. Praying and talking to God was a daily habit, but slowing down to see or hear God's answers, well that was another story.

It wasn't until a bad case of the flu landed me in the bed unable to speak that I became silent enough for the message to come through loud and clear: "Shush! Your prayers haven't gone unanswered, you just aren't still enough to see it."

The memories of how many times I missed seeing my answered prayers became clear once I began taking time early in the morning—after praying—to just sit and be with God with no preplanned agenda.

God had worked wondrously through others to provide for me and my children, consistently without fail, but my eyes were locked on the way I thought it should have happened. I remember asking God to change me and show me how to put Him first and live the fruit of the Spirit by being kinder, loving, faithful, and patient with more self-control. I couldn't even see that God was clearing the path for my new life when people and things of my old life began to leave or be removed.

Today, I'm still on my knees and if there is a need I will ask, but I now completely trust and have faith that God will answer according to His Will, not mine, and I'm happy with His outcomes. God always answers my prayers and His answers always bless me in unimaginable ways.

Take a moment…Be Still and Know

—Jaie Benson

Mission Possible

"Keep me as the apple of Your eye; Hide me under the
shadow of Your wings..." (Psalm 17:8 NKJV)

In despair, I walked through these doors
Asking, what was I there for?
As I looked for the one in charge
I felt the hands of the Almighty at large!
My heart was broken, my spirit beat
The lady said, "You're safe. Please take a seat."
As I listened to the plan of this mission,
It was as though I saw a vision.
So I prayed the cry of this battle
I opened the Bible and felt a rattle.
For the arms of my Father spread before me,
I gasped a breath and asked what can this be?
The answer I heard,
Is in the Lord's Word,
"I am the King."
And, you're under my wing,
For every day, you will fly
Always knowing where and why
Because, you see, the Holy Spirit
Will always be there to hear it.
My mission in life through all the strife
Is to live, love, and be loved
To You my God above.

—Cathi Rumbaugh

Written after accepting Jesus as Lord and Savior in January 2003.

My First Love

"Nevertheless I have somewhat against thee, because thou hast left thy first love." (Revelation 2:4 KJV)

My first teenage crush didn't even know I existed. But every time he walked by me in the hallway I thought I would faint. Every day as I walked in to school those butterflies in the pit of my stomach would return and remain there until I walked out at the end of the day.

I'm all grown up now and I can't even remember my crush's name. It is God who now makes me excited and giddy with nonstop butterflies at the mere thought of Him—and every time I hear His name.

God is the One! He is my First Love. I wake up each day asking Him what He wants to do and He guides my steps in every way, which I obediently follow with joy. During the day I write little love notes on pretty cards and imagine sitting at God's feet as I read them to Him. Before I close my eyes at night, I ask Him to show me how I could have been better, have served greater, and have loved more. I sleep peacefully, eager to open my eyes in the morning anew to work even harder to make Him proud.

When I made God my primary relationship, all of my earthly connections took on a fresh new beautiful loving tone, but they pale in comparison to the love I feel for God, My First Love.

God is waiting with open arms and ready to sweep us off our feet!

—Jaie Benson

Oh How He Loves Us

"For my thoughts are not your thoughts, neither are your
ways my ways, declares the Lord." (Isaiah 55:8 NIV)

When I was a young girl, not even a teenager yet, I became angry with the Lord and took off on the wrong path for my life. It was about twelve years later that I hit rock bottom. When I looked at my life, all I saw was hopelessness, failure, and mistakes. All I could feel was the deep pit of pain and regret. I was a young woman, but I believed the lie that when people added up all of my shortcomings, I was worth nothing. And I contemplated just ending things.

It was a Sunday that my father asked me, once again, to go to church with him and Mom. We went and I felt a deep pull on my heart. I can't remember what the pastor said, but I hung onto every word. When he gave the altar call, I went. I went to the altar a slave to many things, but I stood up a child of Christ. It was like exiting a tomb. I was truly reborn.

In the many years since that day, I have often reflected on what God did when he set me free that day. I reflect on his love. I collect evidence of God's love the way a young bride collects flowers for her bouquet. Like the time I prayed for a fresh, green Christmas wreath and one was given to me. Then there was the time that the home we found was perfect—just for us. There were those evenings I spent at a favorite restaurant, being refreshed and refilled. Finally, there were the times in church when God's presence filled my heart, and the times on my daily walks when I could hear his voice, saying what I needed to hear and what I needed to know to get through the journey another day. Those are the small things, but they mean so much. They are evidence that God sees me—specifically me—and loves me as a unique person.

As I sized up my life as a non-Christian, I came up with a big, fat zero. I did not see the years of healing, joy, and fulfillment that would come after I gave my life to Christ. I was blind. After I gave my heart to Christ, the hope for a good life was perhaps the greatest evidence of my new faith. After becoming a Christian, what I remember most was the recurring message that Christ loved me as a sinner, and that he loved me as his child. When we use human measuring sticks to size ourselves up, we are not using God's wisdom. When we judge others or ourselves to be hopeless, we are listening to the enemy, not to Christ.

When God looks at us, He does not use a yardstick to measure us. When He looks at us, He sees the truth. When He looks at us, He sees a future of blessings if we come to Him, and if we live in obedience and faithfulness. His ways are not our ways (v. 8). His love is perfect. As we strive to get closer to God, we strive for the greatest thing of all—to love like Christ, to sacrifice for others, to forgive great hurts, and to live in the fullness of hope as we exercise our faith.

—Kristen Welch

Power to Create Change

"Therefore be imitators of God [copy Him and follow His example], as well-beloved children [imitate their father]." (Ephesians 5:1 AMP)

The word "create" means to bring into existence: having the power to originate. We all have the power to create —given to us by God, the Creator Himself. That is, in the flesh we create what we like and enjoy; we create what makes us happy. We even create what is necessary to live. Let's look at ourselves spiritually.

Creating new things – Changing old things. Because you and I are made in the image of God, that's something we're always trying to do. But if we're to be successful at it, we need to learn a lesson about it from the Creator Himself. You know, He didn't just come upon creation by accident and say, "Well, what do you know! There's light!" *No!* Before He began to make His universe we can imagine that He first had a desired result—an image He wanted to create—and then He said, *"Let there be light"* (Genesis 1:3 AMP), and light was. If we are going to imitate Him, we're going to have to put the principle of the inner image to work within ourselves as well. "But," you say, "That was God. Surely you don't expect me to try to act like God." I most certainly do. Ephesians 5:1 says to!

If you are a born-again child of Almighty God, He has given you the principle and the power to make permanent changes in your life and in your circumstances through the power of God's Holy Spirit within you. Wow, that's great power!

What you need to use as the basis of the inner image you want to create and for the words you desire to speak is the Word of God, the Holy Bible. The Word has the supernatural power to show us actually what needs to be adjusted in our lives. And if you fill that Word with faith and speak it out, it will work for you to change your life and circumstances. Romans 12:2, is one good place to begin. It tells us to be transformed by the renewing of our mind with new ideals and attitudes so that we may prove for ourselves what is the good and acceptable and perfect will of God [emphasis added].

Therefore, take the challenge –
Find out what real creativity is all about
and start rebuilding yourself and your world today.

—Tancy Elliott

Plugged In

"I have come that they may have life and that they may have it more abundantly." (John 10:10 NKJV)

God is always there for us but we ignore, reject, and put off recognizing all He has for us. We live defeated Christian lives and become satisfied with crumbs when He has a complete meal for us. Our Christian witness is weak and ineffective because we are undernourished. We haven't fed on God's word nor claimed His promises. We are unplugged from the real source of life and become disillusioned in our search for the abundant life.

I tried to achieve the abundant life by staying busy with church activities and being the "Best Mom and Loving Wife."

One day at Bible study a friend shared with me and said "Mae, Jesus just wants all of you fully surrendered to Him in every area of your life; He will take care of the rest." I prayed in my devotions and said "Lord I'm ready to give you every area of my life, but I'm afraid I can't do it without failing." I walked over to my window and saw a pair of redbirds perched in a tree. I said, "Lord I will start praying about every problem and troublesome issue in my life. If the birds fly away before I am finished I will assume this isn't you." To my surprise the birds flew away the minute I whispered "Amen."

I said, "Lord, I am yours—please live your life in and through me." He did, and I received the abundant life and so much more that very afternoon. That was January 1973. I am 80 years old as I write this today and I continue to praise Him for all of His blessings given freely to me.

—Living Abundantly,
Mae Mattingly

Ride Through It (Offended)

"Then Peter came to Jesus and asked, "Lord, how many times
shall I forgive my brother or sister who sins against me? Up
to seven times?" Jesus answered, I tell you, not seven times,
but seventy-seven times." (Matthew 18 21:22 NIV)

When someone offends us, it can be traumatizing. No one likes harsh criticism. The trauma may manifest itself physically as the pain of being stabbed to the quick or like a kick to the stomach. In chronic cases, repeated offenses such as abuse can lead to sickness, depression, or addictive behaviors. God's Word teaches us how to handle offenses in a Godly manner.

When my horse "Annie" spooks, the equivalent of an equine offense, I must ride through it. If I panic, my fear traumatizes the horse more. If I get angry or throw a fit I make a bad situation worse. If I jump off the horse, I do not deal with the issue. Riding a horse is so much like dealing with human insults. You never know when they may be thrown at you! I have learned with practice to ride through the horsey offense.

Sometimes, when I am the recipient of a human insult, I fail miserably and in the heat of the moment repeat the undesirable behavior patterns learned long ago, resident like well-worn tracks in my robot-like brain. I find myself making the offense ten times worse than if I had just "let it go" in the first place. Metaphorically, I have to pick myself up, dust myself off, and pray for the strength next time not to repeat these well learned automatic patterns. Fortunately, the Holy Spirit has revealed to me some of my ingrained bad patterns of behavior—so now I am forewarned as to my likely reaction and more aware of being able to choose not to follow those well-worn tracks.

Sometimes I sense that an offense is Satan's trap to get us to sin, which God seems to allow in order to build our character. God's instruction is crystal clear:

It is to forgive the offence—just as He has forgiven us.
This is the correct and only choice.

I have found it helpful to always take a hard look at myself in the face of offense. Resist the temptation to judge the other person. It is so easy to immediately think "it is their fault" and you are just the poor innocent victim. Talk with yourself to handle it with God's strength in a manner that would please Him. No kicking or screaming (emotional outbursts) or going through the hedge backwards. What might you have been, said, or done to cause it? After all, you cannot change other people. You can only change yourself. Ask for discernment: "Is it appropriate to forgive the offender, love and pray for them and let it go?" Or do you approach them and ask whether you might have offended them and if so to offer your apologies? Ask God for help in letting it go--so you do not handle it like a dog with a bone--chewing away at the insult and letting it pierce you to the marrow. You have made yourself a victim of your circumstances, rather than releasing it.

When I follow this advice, I am filled with that mysterious inner peace and grace, which only God can provide. I experience the freedom to let the offense blow away, like a puff of fractious wind.

—Catherine Ricks Urbalejo

Rise and Live

"For nothing is impossible with God." (Luke 1:37 NIV)

"How could it be, my dear friend, that you will soon be free and flyaway straight to heaven to Jesus and our Heavenly Father?

We've often talked how glorious that will be! We've talked about wanting to wait for the rapture. If we had our choice and could go up together; how wonderful that would be!

Never did I ever know you would become ill enough to possibly make this transition without me so soon.

I will miss you; so if and when you go I can't even imagine how gorgeous heaven will be. The peace and love will be such a reward. The songs the angels sing, I can't even imagine how beautiful they will sound. I wonder, do you think I will be able to sing with them? That is my dream.

So part in peace, and know you certainly were a disciple here on earth, leading people to Christ and being a true ambassador for Jesus.

God also puts us all here for different reasons, so some of my accomplishments will differ from the ones you were blessed with. So my dear, smile on me when I carry out something that pleases our Lord. I'll never say "Good Bye" because we will someday see each other again. Just, "all my love till we meet again."

P.S. — Praise God! A few weeks after I wrote this note for my friend the Lord healed her! She's walking around better than ever continuing her Christian duties—grateful and praising God!

We never know when Jesus is going to step in and change our lives through a miracle. "Never give up" is what I've learned. Jesus will lift us up when we least expect it.

Rise and Live.

—Lynne Brown

Send Me a Song, Lord

"Be still and know that I am God." (Psalm 46:10 NIV)

Send me a song, Lord. Send me a new song. Write upon my heart words I can sing; telling friends of mine of your love divine and how you can set them free. I imagined the Lord might say:

"I died upon Calvary's tree for your sins to set your soul free. Just open your heart and let me come in; I'm your nearest and dearest friend.

Be still and know that I am God (v. 10); I'm as near to you as your heart. I'm near day and night to bear all your strife. Just yield and let me come in.

Each child of God is born with ways to show my love. Just search in your heart for your special way to spread my Holy Word."

You free us from our strife Lord. You free us from our heartaches. You free us in our times of tempting sin. It's so nice to know we have a place to go.

Thank you Lord for those songs that bring peace to our souls.

—Lynne Brown

Sin

"And when he is come, he will reprove the world of sin, and of righteousness, and of judgment." (John 16:8 KJV)

"As far as the east is from the west, so far hath he removed our transgressions from us." (Psalm 103:12 KJV)

When I was younger it was important for me to be viewed by the world as broad-minded. This meant that I believed that homosexuality was acceptable. In addition, I was so centered on the big "I, me, and myself" that I was a staunch believer in a woman's right to choose. Those strong beliefs I held for the majority of my life. How I have changed since those days!

It seemed rather odd at the time, but those convictions began to change over a period of several months. Not because any person lectured me on these issues, but because something inside caused me to change those beliefs. As I have learned more biblical truth, I have come to understand that the gift of the Holy Spirit—promised by Jesus to those who believe on Him—came into my life and, as taught in the Bible, has convicted me of sin. Now I love the person, but hate the sin of homosexuality. Now I know that having an abortion when I was forty- four was wrong. Before I came to truly know the Lord it had rarely bothered me at all. This is my personal witness that the Holy Spirit does indeed reside in me. How blessed I am.

Discernment, a gift of the Holy Spirit that convicts us of sin, comes with accountability. Be wary of becoming a tool of criticism. Be able to forgive yourself just as the Lord has forgiven you for that sin. Do not constantly berate yourself for past sins. By continuing to do so you are mocking the crucifixion where our Lord took all the sins of the world— including yours and mine—on Himself. Who are we to question the ultimate sacrifice made by our Lord Jesus Christ to enable us access to a Holy God.

Have you been convicted of your sins and have you forgiven yourself for them, as your heavenly Father has forgiven you?

—Catherine Ricks Urbalejo

Stains

"My dear children, I write this to you so that you will not sin. But if anybody does sin, we have an advocate with the Father—Jesus Christ, the Righteous one." (1 John 2:1 NIV)

Oh no! I looked at my shirt—spaghetti sauce specks all over the front of it. I thought *why is it that whenever I make spaghetti sauce, red stains can be found on the stove, the wall, and almost always on my clothing? It seems no matter how careful I am, there is always evidence I prepared spaghetti sauce.* There is no hiding it, and sometimes the red specks don't come out in the wash.

As I complained about my shirt, the Holy Spirit reminded me of the story of King David and Bathsheba in 2 Samuel 11 and 12—how David attempted to cover up the stains of his sin. He was home from the war and gave in to temptation as he took Bathsheba, who was another man's wife. Then, in order to cover up his indiscretion, he had her husband, Uriah, come home so that Uriah could be with her. But Uriah was an honorable and loyal man and did not sleep with his wife as David had expected. As a last ditch attempt at covering up his transgression, David gave orders to his general to place Uriah on the battle's front line, assuring that he would die. After Uriah's death, David made Bathsheba his wife. She gave birth to his son, but the child later died. Eventually, the prophet, Nathan, confronted David with a parable about a poor man whose only lamb was taken by a rich man. King David was incensed at this story, condemning "the rich man" to death, failing to recognize his own wrongdoing until Nathan said, "You are the man." Finally, David acknowledged his sin and repented. God forgave him. But, there were still consequences to suffer.

Just as I am cautious when I make spaghetti sauce to avoid stains from getting on everything, King David carefully tried to cover up his sin. Yet—no matter what I do—those little red spots (without fail) appear on something and often, become permanent stains. David resorted to drastic measures, but was still unable to hide his sin. It appeared just like the sauce stains appear and his consequences were

29

severe. Sin has an ugly habit of exposing itself—its stains cannot be hidden. Not for very long, anyway.

We as believers, however, have hope! When we sin and truly repent, we can ask Jesus, who is our "advocate with the Father," for forgiveness. Our heavenly Father is faithful to forgive us. Just like he forgave David, God will forgive us, but we may have to deal with the stains, the consequences resulting from our sin.

—Juanita Adamson

The Fire

"May the favor of the Lord our God rest
upon us." (Psalm 90:17 NIV)

The Monument Fire in our Arizona county a few years ago was a heartrending time for all. It was a week of fear and wonder. Our beautiful canyon forest was severely damaged.

When my parents retired and moved to Sierra Vista, Arizona, they built their home in Stump Canyon. Built on two and a half acres, it was a modest home. Daddy had his chickens and mother had her garden. My children have many memories of the hanging tree, Buttercup, Nibblets, and the fire tanker that was kept on the property. My parents have long passed away and the property belongs to someone else now, but my family and I still have an emotional attachment to the property. So when the fire roared through the canyon, we worried that all the things of the past memories would be gone.

It was several weeks before we could go into the canyon as we no longer owned any property there. The day finally came and as we drove through the destruction the scene took my breath away. The forest my children walked through to and from the bus stop was gone. Before, where there was forest, now you could see through the destruction to the houses that were left and the mountain, but our old house was still there. The property is back to back with the church camp and, surprisingly, very little of the camp property burned. It is located in the middle of all the forest that burned. It was amazing to see how God redirected the fire around the camp. In doing so He saved the property we once owned. It doesn't look the same, but it is still there. We are confident that someday the forest will return. We are also grateful that God was merciful that day and let His "favor rest upon" the camp and our family.

—Sue Walker

The Most Interesting People I Know

"...ye are a chosen generation, a royal priesthood, an
holy nation, a peculiar people; that ye should show forth
the praises of him who hath called you out of darkness
into his marvelous light:" (1 Peter 2:9 KJV)

Various geophysical databases estimate that there are about 7.1 billion people in the world. Amazingly, among those numbers are two of the most interesting people I have ever met—You and Me! Narcissistically speaking, *No*, but in a wonderfully grateful and overwhelming sense of worth.

We are notable works of art. The work of a discriminate Artist who continues to remind us that we are "...fearfully and wonderfully made; [and that His] works are wonderful..." (Psalm 139:14 KJV) [emphasis added]. That same Artist also calls us His peculiar people. Not in the descriptive sense as odd or strange—although some of us may also fall into that category—but as His precious possessions who He carefully guards and protects to carry out His Divine missions in the world. We are His "highly esteemed" private property for whom He gave His own life to protect us from an eternity of death and separation from Himself.

Yes, we who have accepted Jesus Christ as our Lord and Savior are some of the most interesting people I know. Yet, as diligent as we are, we can't get everything right. We fall so short of our potential many times throughout the day. We sometimes disrespect His name and are often fearful to share His love with others. In addition, we all have closets so full of skeletons that we dare not open the door!

That could really make one wonder how a holy God could be so totally enamored with us. But that's what Amazing Grace is all about, isn't it – Hallelujah!

—Phyllis Andrews

The Rainbow After the Storm

"Restore to me the joy of your salvation and grant me a
willing spirit to sustain me." (Psalm 51:12 NIV)

In 1947 a baby girl was born. Everyone in the whole family and extended families were thrilled. I was the third girl out of six grandchildren who were aged six to ten. So a new baby girl was much welcomed and loved. They named me Lynne Darlene Peninger.

My father was especially proud of me. He carried me everywhere and enjoyed me as I grew from year to year, that is until I turned six and started first grade. Our little town of Barnsdall, Oklahoma, had 300 people so kindergarten didn't exist.

When school started, it was then discovered that I was left-handed. Daddy was always so busy, but when he noticed I was using my left hand as I practiced my numbers at the table, he hollered so loudly I nearly fell out of my chair. He said, "Why are you using your left hand!" He was screaming so loud I couldn't think and fear filled my entire soul. Mother came running and said "Oh Millard, leave her alone, she's making good grades." Then she reminded him of several people in her family who were left-handed, smart, and extremely talented artists. "I don't care, no child of mine is going to be left-handed and stupid," he hollered. I'll never forget the hurt and shame I felt. I buried my head in my folded arms, too afraid to move. Mother cried and left the room after she argued "She's not stupid, leave her alone." She turned and left the room praying "Oh Jesus."

Daddy picked me up and held me as he sat in my chair. He then placed me hard on his lap repeating, "No kid of mine is going to be stupid." He then put my pencil in my right hand and said, "Now write!" I remember struggling, and as a letter and/or number was written backwards—which was 90% of the time—he spanked me or slapped me. This went on for what seemed to be an eternity. Night after night mother cried and begged for him to stop. Even my brothers cried and stayed in their rooms with their doors closed. Each day I struggled.

My teacher was also very upset and tried talking to my father, but to no avail.

After a while I started writing my numbers and letters correctly. Once in a while they would go in the wrong direction, but my teacher lovingly helped me.

As a result of the abuse my father put me through I was ultimately diagnosed with attention deficit hyperactivity disorder (ADHD) and severe concentration and retention problems.

My mother stopped the abuse one night as Daddy and I were working. I heard her say—with the broom in her hands raised in the air— "Millard Peninger, if you continue abusing my baby girl I will beat you with this broom." He responded, "Oh Miriam, that's ridiculous." "Okay," she said, and starting hitting him with the broom. Needless to say she beat him into submission, "Okay, okay!" he said. From then on I went back to my left hand with a little struggle. I was a happy little girl even though I was left with the learning disorders. I still struggle to this day from the disorders, but I've accomplished so much as a normal adult.

Jesus took me as a little girl and healed me of feeling stupid and inadequate. It took a long time, but Jesus has never stopped healing me. I claim it every day and believe with all my faith. He helped me through two years of college and much more. I accept all the miracles he has helped me through. I feel that the struggle of learning is my testimony. That with Jesus I can continue to learn as I have been. Taking more time to learn is a blessing, because doctors told my mother I could be retarded, but "Praise God," I'm not. Struggles make us strong and as I think of all I have accomplished in my life, I consider myself normal and full of the Grace of God. I am healed! It lets me know I wouldn't be who I am today had I not gone through the hardships with my dad. And yes, as an adult, I have forgiven him, realizing he didn't know better. He was taught this from his parents and was only carrying out the tradition of what he had been taught, whether right or wrong.

I pray that sharing this will help someone who has or is going through struggles that seem unfair or too hard to go through. First

Corinthians 10:13 NIV says "And, God is faithful, he will not let you be tempted beyond what you can bear."

I've learned that there's always a miracle on the other side of difficult circumstances, as long as we keep Jesus in charge.

Look for the rainbow after the storm.

—Lynne Brown

The Walk is Winding

"As obedient children, do not conform to the evil desires you
had when you lived in ignorance. But just as he who called
you is holy, so be holy in all you do." (1 Peter 1:14-15 NIV)

From age seven to present Grandma Walker has been my spiritual compass, even though she died in 1989. In 1950, when we were living with my grandmother at her ranch near Naco, Arizona, my dad moved us to Ft. Huachuca, the military post in nearby Sierra Vista. While attending third grade I would go to a friend's house after school for catechism. After three weeks, my parents said I couldn't go to his home anymore, because we were Protestant, not Catholic. So, I attended chapel on post until we moved to Fry, Arizona, in 1954.

While attending my local elementary school, I noticed that the teacher of my fifth, sixth, and seventh grade combined class was also the Baptist pastor at a church where a friend of mine attended. He invited me to go on a few Sundays.

I was "moved" by the Holy Spirit to answer a call to the altar one Sunday and the congregation was excited for all of the children who came forward to receive Jesus Christ as Savior! We were to return to the church on Thursday evening to be baptized. However, that Thursday morning the pastor read us the riot act at school and punctuated it by throwing a chair across the front of the classroom! From that moment I was determined not to go to the baptism. However, my friend came from the church and got me. We arrived late and as we entered the back of the church I saw another friend being dunked under the water and I immediately reversed course! Accordingly, I was not baptized until I was twenty-one when I married an Episcopal girl and there was no dunking involved—I've since been immersed at my local church and survived.

I've learned that sometimes the Lord leads us on a straight and narrow path and at other times it is winding and doubles back.

We need to just keep walking—for the destination is a glorious reward!

—David Walker

"Unclean, Unclean"

"As far as the east is from the west, so far hath He removed our transgressions from us." (Psalm 103:12 KJV)

Under Old Testament Law, a person who was pronounced by the priest to be infected with the disease of leprosy was cut off from his family and friends, his business, and also ostracized from the temple worship. Under the law, the disease of leprosy was a symbol of sin and God's displeasure with the infected person. To add to their shame, such a person had to wear a torn garment as a sign of his grief and sorrow for his apparent sin. He had to live with other lepers and go about with his head uncovered as a sign of his humility. In addition, to acknowledge his sin and warn others of his condition, he had to cover his upper lip and cry "unclean, unclean" to passersby. As you probably have already learned, the horrible consequence of leprosy is that the leprous person's physical features and limbs decay and ultimately fall off. It's described as a living death.

As I studied various referenced verses of Scripture and related commentaries all I could say was "Praise God for Jesus and His prevenient grace!" He knew that a diagnosis and pronouncement by a priest—when a person was no longer considered leprous—was not the long-term fix for the sinful nature of mankind. We would still be walking around with our upper lip covered and exclaiming "unclean, unclean," if Jesus Christ had not given his life on the cross to pay the penalty for our sins. However, if you are struggling with sin in your life, be confident in the fact that God can remove your sin from you "as far as the east is from the west (v. 12)," which, scientifically speaking, is the largest measure the earth can render.

In effect, it is an unending cycle of God's compassion on those who willingly come to him in submission to His will and His way.

—Phyllis Andrews

Where There is Life

"But I trust in your unfailing love; my heart rejoices
in your salvation. I will sing the LORD's praise, for
he has been good to me." (Psalm 13:4-6 NIV)

In spite of the warm winter we experienced last year, our sago palm froze. When we saw the frozen fronds, victims of the few days the temperatures dipped to freezing, we regrettably remembered we had forgotten to cover it. We decided that we would pull it out of the planter and replace it with another. However, we never got around to replacing it although the brown fronds greeted us every time we came in or out of the front door.

One early spring morning, we noticed a little emerald green colored frond forming at the center of the brown dead-looking stump. A few days later, more fronds began to uncurl their little tips. The palm was not dead; it was growing. There was life that we couldn't see until it started to turn green.

Often, when we pray for the salvation of our loved ones and they show little or no evidence of ever accepting Christ, we want to give up on them. We think *why are we wasting our time praying and telling them about Jesus?* But remember that God's unfailing love never gives up. Like our little palm, as long as there is life, there is hope that they will finally make the right decision and give their hearts and lives to Jesus.

Several years ago, my husband and I took our nephew into our home. He went to church with us, but never really made a commitment to serve God. When he moved out, he quit going to church. We continued to pray for him hoping he would surrender to Jesus, but there was no sign he was even vaguely interested.

After he married and he and his wife had their first child, he answered the Holy Spirit's call on his life. Fifteen years later, he is still serving God and is active in his church and community. He trusts God's unfailing love and rejoices in His salvation. He thanks Jesus for his family, his job, and everything he is and has. He knows that God has been good to him even though he ran from Him for several years.

Like our sago palm, there was no evidence of life in our nephew— not any spiritual life that we could see. But, the Holy Spirit saw what we couldn't and never gave up on him. Today, he is in love with Jesus and is a godly example to his children and friends. He is one of God's trophies.

Don't give up on those you are praying for—Jesus doesn't give up. In His perfect timing, they will open their hearts and receive the Lord as Savior. You'll see!

—Juanita Adamson

~ Section 2 ~
THE THRONE OF GRACE

"Let us then approach God's throne of grace with confidence,
so that we may receive mercy and find grace
to help us in our time of need."

(Hebrews 4:16 NIV)

Another "Seed and Weed" Story

"...study to show thyself approved unto God, a
workman that needeth not to be ashamed, rightly
dividing the word of truth." (2 Timothy 2:15 KJV)

A weed at the edge of our patio had grown to over thirty-six inches tall as a result of the torrential Arizona monsoon rains during July. One could even muse that it was just about big enough to support Christmas ornaments.

It stood stately in place due to the missing presence of the gentleman who takes care of our landscaping and my reluctance—mixed with a measure of procrastination—to simply pull it up from its royal position. There's no way to tell how long its roots or seed had waited under the rocks for the blessing of the downpours.

Continuing my story, I finally headed out the door to remove this weed that had become an eyesore. I'm almost certain that my actions pleased my neighbors tremendously. This scenario also made me realize how easily our spiritual wellbeing can be jeopardized when we sometimes allow the seed of God's word to land in the rocky soil of our everyday complacency and busyness.

We often read our daily Bible devotion, write a few notes in the margin, and then pray just long enough to "satisfy" what we believe is our need for communication with God each day. Then, as the ultimate plight of that giant weed was, the Word of God can be yanked up out of our heart and mind with only the firm twist and pull of the daily trials of life—- because its roots were not deeply planted and nourished.

—Phyllis Andrews

Blessed, Blessed, Blessed

"Rejoice evermore. Pray without ceasing. In everything
give thanks: for this is the will of God in Christ Jesus
concerning you." (1 Thessalonians 5:16–18 KJV)

On many Thursdays at a local nursing home an 83-year old volunteer can be heard proclaiming in a loud voice, "In everything give thanks (v. 18)," as she testifies of God's goodness in her life. Even though her walk is becoming hesitant, her eyesight dimming, her hearing fading, and her overall health waning, she never fails to declare her gratitude of God's blessings. Based on the world's standards, these blessings are the simple things we often unappreciatively take for granted. For example, finding enough change to ride the bus (she no longer drives), receiving cookies to satisfy her sweet tooth or a book she wanted to read, being asked to dinner, or receiving an unexpected visit or ride from a friend or a relative. To her it doesn't matter what it may be, because she finds joy in all things and thanks God for them.

Her life has not been easy—she endured divorce and then remarried the same man but, at the same time, was able to fulfill her life-long dream of going to Africa to teach. As a widow, she has lived with family and most recently was blessed to be able to move into a newly constructed apartment for seniors. She is a talented pianist, playing for whom she loves most—Jesus. She lives a simple life, but makes it her priority to praise God for all things. She never complains or talks about her illnesses. When asked how she is, she always exclaims "blessed, blessed, blessed!" Her excitement and unadulterated appreciation of God's love is reflected in the sparkle of her eyes and her tireless smile.

I often wonder whether she is aware of how much of an inspiration and a wonderful example she is to others. What a positive effect she has on those people who come in contact with her as she praises God for even the little blessings she receives.

The Bible tells us to rejoice, to pray without ceasing, and to give thanks for everything. But somehow we forget. Too often we occupy our time with fussing and complaining, wanting our lives to be different, instead of being thankful for everything and doing "the will of God in Christ Jesus (v. 18)."

—Juanita Adamson

Chain of God

*"And we know that all things work together for good
to them that love God, to them who are the called
according to his purpose." (Romans 8:28 KJV)*

Opening the door of the mobile home, I stepped in. I could barely make out the vague shapes of the furniture; the darkness was so intense. I called out her name as I stumbled around looking for a light switch. A weak voice responded from the darkness. "I am here." The voice appeared to be coming from somewhere on the floor. I peered through the darkness and finally spied her. She was lying on her stomach, writhing in agony.

For some reason, I had been led to visit my friend that particular day. I believe this was at the nudging of the Holy Spirit. She had recently had surgery for cancer requiring the removal of her lower intestine. She lived alone with no income and few friends. She had been attending our cowboy church prior to the surgery.

Switching on the light, I managed to get her up on the couch. I rubbed her stomach. It was as hard as a rock. She told me that she could not eat anything without vomitting. I suggested that perhaps we should call 911. "No," she responded obstinately; her face etched with pain. "I do not want to go to hospital. I have spent too much time there already," she whimpered. "Besides it is only gas," she said, pointing to her hardened stomach which protruded grotesquely from her pitiful, skeletal-like body.

After continued rubbing, which seemed to give her some relief, but no success in convincing her to call 911, I returned home very unsettled. I told my husband about the incident. He immediately pointed out that I should return; that she might die. His remark worried me more. I hastened back to the mobile home and again suggested that we should call 911. She remained resistant to this suggestion but did agree to my calling her hospital surgeon in Tucson, Arizona, to procure advice. I reached for the phone.

In the meantime, unbeknownst to me, my husband, who was alarmed by my remarks, called another church member who again—unbeknownst to me—called 911.

Much to my surprise and great relief an ambulance miraculously appeared at the door. I hastily put down the phone, as the paramedics stepped inside the door. She was not pleased to see them, refusing to go with them. She thought I had called them. I assured her I had not. The paramedics, after some heroic persuasive efforts, convinced her—albeit reluctantly—to go with them. With considerable relief, as it appeared that the matter was now out of my hands, I watched the ambulance depart for the local hospital.

Our pastor, hearing about the incident from yet another church member, immediately went to the hospital. He was informed that she had a serious stomach blockage and would have died had she not received immediate treatment.

God had worked supernaturally through a chain of people to resolve a difficult situation and save her life. How thankful we should be that God is in control!

—Catherine Ricks Urbalejo

Choices

"Finally, brethren, whatsoever things are true, whatsoever
things are honest, whatsoever things are just, whatsoever
things are pure, whatsoever things are lovely, whatsoever
things are of good report; if there be any virtue, and if there
be any praise, think on these things." (Philippians 4:8 KJV)

"What hat should I wear to the Women of Grace Writers' meeting?"
I pondered. The question reverberated in my head, wobbling back
and forth between two choices: "Should I select my baseball horse
cap, bejeweled with multiple, colorful, and generally gaudy pins of the
various states I had travelled to? Or should I choose my authentic,
dusty, cowgirl hat which had seen numerous horseback rides to a
variety of locations in Cochise County, Arizona? I think I will go with
authenticity," I muttered to myself. The decision was made and a feeling
of great relief swarmed over me.

Making a decision between these two— albeit trivial—choices
caused me to ponder more critical decisions than the mere selection
of a hat. Of course the most important choice we ever made was our
decision to follow Jesus Christ as Lord and Savior. But how do we go
about making godly decisions as believers in our daily walk when the
flaming arrows of the devil are bombarding us from every quarter?
As believers, we have been equipped with several tools to enable us to
make wise choices "IF" we choose to do so.

Believers have the Bible—the inspired Word of God—as their
instruction manual. Reading the Bible and ingraining the word of
God in your heart and mind provides a godly filter through which one
can strain our circumstances. The Holy Spirit, the promised gift to all
believers, convicts us of sin and points us to the right choice. Together
with the gift of discernment and heart felt prayer to our heavenly
Father we have all the tools necessary to make wise choices that will
be grounded in God's wisdom.

It will be challenging. After all, since the dawn of creation and Adam and Eve's initial sin in the Garden of Eden, man has been spiritually and physically disfigured by his wrong choices. Choose what is right based on God's wisdom, not your own. Jesus never said it would be easy, but the promised rewards are inner strength, peace, and the blessed hope of eternal life with our Lord and Savior, Jesus Christ.

—Catherine Ricks Urbalejo

Complete and Unconditional Surrender

"Truly, truly, I say to you, unless one is born again, he
cannot see the kingdom of God." (John 3:3 NASB)

On September 2, 1945, the U.S.S. Missouri was docked in Tokyo
Harbor for the signing of a complete and unconditional surrender of
the Empire of Japan to end World War II. The newsreel, as it was called
at that time, recorded and filmed the entire proceeding, which was later
in movie theaters. I was five years old and remember the sight of the
Emperor of Japan and some of his government officials and generals,
dressed in black tuxedos with tails and black top hats, coming aboard
the Missouri to a table where General Douglas MacArthur was seated
with his staff. It was there where the documents were signed that began
a long period of American occupation of Japan. To this day, Japan is
one of the United States' strongest allies.

Close to 1,900 years earlier, a bright young Pharisee, trained in the
Jewish laws by the highly respected teacher Gamaliel, was persecuting
and killing the people of "The Way." This was a name given to
Christians at that time. This young Pharisee had not accepted Jesus as
the awaited Messiah and considered Him to be committing blasphemy.
This zealot was Saul of Tarsus:

> "Now Saul, still breathing threats and murder against the
> disciples of the Lord, went to the high priest, and asked
> for letters from him to the synagogues at Damascus, so
> that if he found any belonging to the Way, both men and
> women, he might bring them bound to Jerusalem. As he was
> traveling, it happened that he was approaching Damascus,
> and suddenly a light from heaven flashed around him; and
> he fell to the ground and heard a voice saying to him, 'Saul,
> Saul, why are you persecuting me?'
>
> And he said, 'Who are you, Lord?' And He said, 'I am
> Jesus whom you are persecuting, but get up and enter

the city, and it will be told you what you must do'"
(Acts 9: 1–6 NASB).

The rest of Acts, Chapter 9, describes the relief on the minds of Jesus' disciples—similar to what had to be on the minds of the Jews in Europe at the death of Adolph Hitler.

Let us discuss the meaning of the three key words in the title above: "complete," "unconditional," and "surrender." To "surrender" is to "give up one's self, pride, possessions, influence or emotions." "Complete" is what is known as an absolute. One cannot do any more. No more is possible. "Unconditional" means that we cannot add anything to the word to modify or change it. It is, also, an absolute. Therefore, a complete and unconditional surrender means we can hold nothing back. To repent is to forget the old ways and live, totally, by the new way of Jesus. However, the real question is: "Which one, God or the devil, is the Truth and which one is a counterfeit?" Since the devil cannot win on absolutes, he deals in deception. God's absolute laws have not changed. And He promised His chosen people a Messiah (Savior) who would not change the Law but fulfill it by standing in as the only perfect sacrifice for those sins.

While we can be "saved" by confessing and repenting of our sins and accepting God's perfect sacrifice, Jesus, as our Lord and Savior, we will not know all that God has for us until we make a complete and unconditional surrender to the will of Jesus Christ. "Truly I say to you, unless you are converted and become like children, you will not enter the kingdom of heaven" (Matthew 18: 3, NASB).

Jesus doesn't ask us to check our brain at the door. He asks us to completely and unconditionally surrender ourselves to the plan He has for us. He used Paul in mighty ways, but that would have been impossible without Paul's spirit being broken and his determination to live for Jesus.

We cannot swim with one foot on the shore.

—Jerry Hatfield

Dealing With Guilt

"Have mercy on me…" (Psalm 51:1a NASB)

Guilt is a necessary step in restoring a right relationship with God after we have sinned. If we are aware of our sins, this process could happen several times a day.

From the creation of man—when in Genesis 1:26 (NASB), God said: "Let Us make man in Our image"—to the time when man sinned: "When the woman saw that the tree was good for food…she took from its fruit and ate; and she gave also to her husband with her, and he ate" (Genesis 3:6 NASB), man had lived in a right relationship with God. Thereafter, man was guilt-ridden for he knew he had sinned. He was ashamed and wanted to hide from God. From that time on, the entire Bible is about how God would redeem man back to a right relationship with Himself. What is important for us to know is that we still have a sin nature and therefore need redemption.

Before the advent of Jesus, man had to deal with his guilt differently than we do now. King David, the second of the three kings who ruled the combined nations of Judah and Israel and who was described as "a man after God's own heart," had been handpicked by God to replace King Saul who had disobeyed God (see I Samuel 16:1-23). The covenant between God and David is recorded in II Samuel 7:4-17. David had a special relationship with God and was revered by his people. However, David would commit a grave sin. Though his soul would be saved, his earthly life would not be the same. How David deals with his guilt and how God restores him is a critical lesson for us all. Instead of David leading his army into battle as he had done many times before, he remained behind, placing himself in a position to be tempted. David succumbed to his desire for the beautiful, married, Bathsheba. This resulted in the birth of a son.

At the death of David's infant son, he did what we all should do when we have sinned. He repented, followed God's proper ordinances and prayed for God's forgiveness and restoration.

His prayer of repentance in Psalm 51 contains some of the most profound statements of our relationship to God found anywhere in the Bible.

Verse 1- "Have mercy on me....blot out my transgressions."

Verse 2- "Wash me....from my iniquity; cleanse me from my sin."

Verse 3- "My sin is ever before me."

Verse 4- "Against you, you only, have I sinned."

Verse 5- "In sin did my mother conceive me."

Verse 6- "You teach me wisdom in the secret heart."

Verse 7- "Wash me and I will be whiter than snow."

Verse 10- "Create in me a clean heart, O God, and renew a right spirit within me."

Verse 11- "Take not your Holy Spirit from me."

Verse 12- "Restore to me the joy of Your salvation."

Verse 15- "O Lord, open my lips, and my mouth will declare your praise."

Verse 17- "...a broken and contrite heart, O God, you will not despise."

David understood that it was not what he did,
but what God did in him.

If you are now laboring under guilt, you must understand what causes it, where it comes from, the important truths of Psalm 51, and the final solution of complete surrender to Jesus as your Lord and Savior.

Then, and only then, will guilt serve its intended purpose in your life.

—Jerry Hatfield

Death Grip

"Forget the former things; do not dwell on the past.
See, I am doing a new thing! Now it springs up; do you
not perceive it? I am making a way in the desert and
streams in the wasteland." (Isaiah 43:18–19 NIV)

The year two thousand and three marked the 50th anniversary of the introduction of the iconic Corvette. In recognition of this event, a limited number of special red collectible Corvettes were manufactured. A colleague of mine, an avid lover of Corvettes, purchased one with glee. He was heard to say that no one would be able to pry the keys from his fingers even on his deathbed. Today I was reminded of that colleague while I was listening to a television evangelist, Charles Stanley, preaching on things, people, or past hurts we simply will or cannot let go of. The essence of the sermon was that believers should seek to release themselves from a death grip on worldly possessions. After all, you will not be taking them with you when you leave this world. There is no quicker way to destroy a relationship with a loved one than to hold on so tightly that you smother or control the person you profess to love. They will most likely pull away from you and even remove themselves from you entirely. God gave us the right to make our own choices. We should do likewise and give that loved one their freedom and never try to control another person.

How difficult it is to let go of an offense or hurt. We can carry childhood traumas for decades. One of the saddest stories I have heard was from a friend of mine, who as a child, was abused by a priest over a period of many years. The priest even used the Bible itself as a tool to intimidate her into submission. How sad that to this day—decades later—she cannot forgive him. Sadder still is the fact that she cannot pick up a Bible and read it or even hear the name of Jesus without remembering that abuse. How important, and yet how difficult, to let such hurts go. But what is the answer? We are to pray to God that He will give us the strength to release our death grip on whatever we have taken hold of with such a ferocious tenacity. It has become a stumbling block between God and us—be it a worldly possession, an earthly relationship or a "hurt" that has victimized us from our past. It grows like a cancer, piercing our soul and becoming more embedded in our being as the days, months and years pass. It can actually become part of our actual identity.

Therefore, search your heart to see if you have a death grip on something that is not pleasing to God, as disclosed in His Word. Come to the throne of grace and ask for His help in releasing it.

Crucify it and let it go!

—Catherine Ricks Urbalejo

Derelict or Divine?

"Be not forgetful to entertain strangers: for thereby some
have entertained angels unawares." (Hebrews 13:2 KJV)

Derelict, *n*. "A property thrown away; a person or thing
abandoned as worthless; as, the streets were full of shabby
derelicts." [3]

"Hmmm." I had encountered many such as this on the streets of
Washington, DC, while employed there for twenty-one years.

On February 14, 1980, my day into work was pretty consistent
with the norm: Carpool drop off for a speedy walk down to 12th and
Pennsylvania avenues. Then a quick-right turn down the sidewalk
to the Jerusalem Deli to mingle in a short lineup of other morning
travelers for bagels and other assortments before beginning the work
day. As I was making that short jaunt to the deli—on Valentine's Day,
no less—I noticed a man dressed in many layers of unmatched clothing.
His head was bowed toward the pavement and his knitted cap was
pulled down so low on his head that it obscured most of his face. His
hands were in his pockets as he sauntered toward me. I quickly ducked
into the deli, inaudibly mumbling something about how he probably
was going to ask me for money, I would be late for work if I stopped,
yada, yada, yada. However, as my turn came to order my standard plain
bagel—untoasted and with cream cheese—my heart reasoned that
this man was probably hungry too, so I ordered a second bagel in a
separate bag.

My office was directly across the avenue from the deli and that's
when I noticed that "the man" had already crossed to the median and
was waiting for the light to turn to continue his walk to the other side.
I mused, "If he comes close to me at the corner, I'll ask him if he's
hungry."

---

[3] Webster's New Twentieth Century Dictionary, Unabridged, Second Edition,
1975, 490

Now you probably can write the rest of this story—Yes, I ran directly into him at the corner, and he gratefully responded, "Sure," when I asked if he was hungry. Yet what troubled me the rest of that day was that he didn't reach desperately for the bag of food as one would have expected, but he slightly cupped his hands as he held them out to receive the bag of food—almost as one would do to catch water for drinking. Also most unusual, was that his hands were spotless! There was no sign of street dirt on his hands or fingernails, and when he raised his head to respond to me, I was amazed to see that his eyes were not blood-shot with evidence of stress from lack of sleep or a damaging life style. They were the brightest and clearest crystal-blue I had ever seen!

Whoa! What manner of man was this? Derelict or Divine?

What I've learned from that encounter—and still know for sure— is that we are called to eagerly reach out in love to "the nations." Not just to a select few who meet our standards of acceptability. That is, what we may call "DERELICT," or common or worthless, may be a "DIVINE ministering spirit (see Hebrews 1:14 KJV)" sent from God to guide us into our destiny and life's work for the Kingdom.

—Phyllis Andrews

Heartfelt

"God is spirit and his worshipers must worship in
the Spirit and in truth." (John 4:24 NIV)

It's Sunday morning, time to be in church praising the Lord. The worship team is primed with songs especially selected for the day—the congregation stands to worship God. Soon, I am caught up in the beat of the music, but giving little thought to the lyrics. It was a startling discovery to learn that at times I have been guilty of singing by rote. It seems that my worship, to my chagrin, has not always involved my heart, but only memorized words and phrases. On autopilot, so to speak.

Recently, the nursing home ministry team began a series of devotions based on the old hymns. We were tasked to study the writers' lives as well as what the words of their hymns meant to them and, more significantly, what those lyrics mean to us personally. My first assignment was an eye opener. Wow! I learned that although I have sung many of the old hymns numerous times throughout the years, I had been singing without reflecting on the lyrics. I didn't know what the words meant to the writer and they certainly held little or no meaning for me. They were just lines to a song—words to repeat.

I wondered how I could truly be worshipping in the 'Spirit and in truth" if I didn't even know what I was singing. After careful study and prayer, the Holy Spirit convicted me of inattention—of just singing, but not considering the words; of not making them heart knowledge, instead of just head knowledge. As the result of the Holy Spirit's intervention in this area of my life, I have become more careful to ponder the words I sing. I have found a closer, deeper understanding of my relationship with Jesus each time those words pass my lips.

Often I think, "if only I could worship like the angels, who are in the very presence of God." Since I know that is not possible, I have decided that I want the words of each hymn and each chorus to be my personal prayer of gratitude and love. And, even though the sound of my voice may not be aesthetically pleasing, I want to sing words felt by my heart in honor of God.

I have come to realize that worship should be part of our daily lives and not just an activity we engage in thirty minutes on Sunday mornings. Worship must become a way of life for each of us, as we seek to glorify our Savior.

—Juanita Adamson

Help, Lord

"…come unto the throne of grace, that we may obtain
mercy, and find grace to help…" (Hebrews 4:16pp KJV)

It was one of those days when even the slightest annoyance threw me
for a loop. Each news cast had provoked a murmuring and discontented
heart that sought to give judgmental expression to the world's self-
centered, sin-biased politics. My attitude was not acceptable. Children,
staff, neighbors, community folks and state authorities need the witness
of Christ in me – the hope of glory, the help of mankind.

So I took my sorry attitude to the Lord. "Father, I've come to the
throne of grace for help. Please, help me, Lord!" "That's not what you
get at the throne of grace," I sensed He whispered. I was in shock!
"*WHAT??!!* Lord, if I can't come to You, where can I go for help!?" I
was undone.

Re-reading Hebrews 4:16, I saw that the overly-provoking
annoyances were because I had failed to receive the Lord's new-every-
day mercies. God's grace and mercy are consistently poured forth and
unendingly available from Him. To receive help, I presented myself
before Him, and without measure, He doused me with the fresh
anointing of His grace and of His mercy. The annoyances became
issues of prayer. The blessed gifts of His mercy and grace settled my
troubled heart. Immediately I was renewed, refilled and refreshed.
Father's mercy and grace was the very help I needed. The Lord's 24/7,
open-door policy allows me entrance at any time, even (and especially)
at my weakest moment. It allows me to be fully restored with His
perpetually available mercy and grace—outside of which, I learned,
there is no help.

—Ana J. Lucore

Help Me With My Unbelief

"And straightway the father of the child cried out, and said with tears, Lord, I believe; help thou mine unbelief." (Mark 9:24 KJV)

When I was just about to give up, I believe I heard that beautiful small still voice whispering in my ear, "Jaie, you are believing in the wrong things dear, and according to your faith, your life is happening unto you. When will you believe what I say about you and your life? When will you see what I see when I look at you?"

As I opened my Bible, the Scriptures began to leap off of the page! The very same verses I had read before were now penetrating my heart and not just lying on the surface of my mind. It felt like I was being introduced to the Truth for the very first time.

I felt immense joy as I read: "I can do all things through Christ who strengthens me (see Philippians 4:13)! With God "all" things are possible (see Matthew 19:26)! God has not given me the Spirit of fear...I was given power, love and a sound mind (see 2 Timothy 1:7)."

Daily I prayed and asked God to help me erase those repeated messages from my childhood; that I would never amount to much and that I would never succeed or go far. My faith increased daily and the more I believed the Word of God, the more the old tapes began to disappear and have less and less control over me.

Today my life reflects my new mind and my new heart. A mind that believes and finally agrees with God's plans for my life and a heart that loves Him and is filled with gratitude for the never-ending love He has for me.

Believe what God says and watch Him make all things new!

—Jaie Benson

It's Real

"The Spirit Himself [thus] testifies together with our own spirit, [assuring us] that we are children of God." (Romans 8:16 AMP)

Every laundry day my mother would "treat" us to her personal concert of numerous hymns. We mused that she sang the entire hymn book as she washed the family clothes in that old ringer washing machine. One such song was "IT'S REAL."[4] The first couple of lines are: "Oh, how well do I remember how I doubted day by day, for I did not know for certain that my sins were washed away..."

Mom knew all of the verses and—often with tears flowing from her eyes—when she got to the chorus her voice would swell and resonate up the basement steps from the laundry room and throughout the entire house—"...Praise God, [all my] doubts are settled, for I know, I know it's real."

I was baptized as a Christian at thirteen years old, but when I was not quite twenty, I asked God in my prayer if I was really "saved from my sins," meaning was I really going to heaven when I died. Not long after that impromptu prayer I had a dream in which I saw myself climbing a ladder to heaven. When I reached the top I was able to look over into the most beautiful scene imaginable. I saw colors and light and beauty that cannot be adequately described. When I awakened, I discerned that God had answered my prayer, assuring me of my salvation in that unbelievable dream.

Everyone who has sincerely accepted Jesus Christ as the Savior and Lord of their life can also have that same assurance—without question—but not necessarily in a dream. The Bible, the very Word of God, gives us that assurance, along with the unction of the Holy Spirit in our lives. For example, the title Scripture above reminds us that "the Spirit of God assures us that we are children of God." The Apostle Paul also wrote in 2 Corinthians 5:5 (AMP) – "Now He who has fashioned

---

[4] "It's Real" by Homer L. Cox, 1907, Public Domain; www.hymnary.org

us ...for this very thing is God, Who also has given us the [Holy] Spirit as a guarantee [of the fulfillment of His promise]." We further read a wonderful prayer that our Lord prayed on our behalf to His Father, before our Lord's ascension into heaven. He said, "Father, I will that they also, whom thou hast given me, be with me where I am; that they may behold my glory ..." (John 17:24 KJV).

I wait with joyful anticipation of that day, because "Praise God, I also know it's real" – You can too!

—Phyllis Andrews

It's Time to Forgive

"...Lord, how oft shall my brother sin against me, and
I forgive him? Till seven times? Jesus saith unto him...
Until seventy times seven...The servant therefore fell down,
and worshipped him, saying, Lord, have patience with me,
and I will pay thee all." (Matthew 18: 21–22, 26 KJV)

Remember when...? That's a question we hear a lot nowadays. Reminiscing with family and friends, we browse through holidays-gone-by, enjoying the memories until inevitably we stumble across the memories we would rather forget. Suddenly the pain comes rushing back. The sting of a parent's criticism, the broken promise of a friend, the rejections, the disappointments, the heartaches...

What should we do with memories like that? Do you have to drag them along, like so much baggage, from year to year? No, we can leave them behind. In fact, we *must* leave them behind. And there's only one way to do it—through forgiveness. I remember when I was at my parent's 50th wedding anniversary...what a great time and to think they were married that long. However, a member of the family made a derogatory remark towards me and my husband that devastated me. Well, I carried that hurt for many years until God dealt with me through the power of His Holy Spirit and I was able to forgive that person. Forgiving someone sounds like a simple thing to do. Yet, few of us actually do it. We treat forgiveness as if it was one of life's additional options, something we can take or leave alone. But it's a basic requirement of every believer. In fact, as far as God is concerned, unforgiveness is wickedness. And in Matthew 18, Jesus tells a parable that illustrates the terrible consequences of unforgiveness. The parable concerns a servant who owed his lord a debt equivalent to millions of dollars. When the debt came due, he pleaded with his master, "Lord, have patience with me and I will pay thee all (v. 26)." His master was so moved that he forgave the debt! Soon after, that same servant sought a man who owed him money. Finding him unable to pay, he ignored the man's pleas for mercy and had him thrown into prison. When his lord heard about it, he called him a wicked servant and delivered him to the tormentors until he paid all that was due.

The petty resentments between husband and wife, between brother and sister, and between friends are so frivolous. *Beware!* Those are the kinds of debts Satan uses to torment you. After all, Jesus paid off a mountain of debts for you. You can be generous about the debts of others. Allow God to reveal the unforgiveness in you and, as you are remembering, make it a time to also forgive and release it.

—Tancy Elliott

Kingdom Marathon

"Do you not know that those who run in a race all
run but one receives the prize? Run in such a way that
you may obtain it." (2 Corinthians 9:24 NKJV)

The decision is ours to enter this "race." It begins the day of our salvation when we pray and invite Jesus to give us a new heart with Him in it. There are well-marked roads. As we travel the narrow road to the Kingdom with other believers, we learn lessons. God equips us with opportunities to learn what we need to know. He gives a life manual called "The Holy Bible" and the Holy Spirit to teach and direct us. He also places people with wisdom to help us understand His Word.

Keep running the race.

There are rough and rocky roads; there are no mistakes that cannot be corrected—only lessons to be learned. We build our endurance by a process of trial and error. Repentance is revealed through our behavior and attitude.

Keep running the race.

As the marathon race for the prize continues, there will be weather conditions—sometimes stormy with temptations, obstacles, enemy confrontations, and distractions on the sidelines. We must remember the "Son" is our holy light and He will hold us, embrace us, and teach us His Father's will. The Holy Spirit will guide us and encourage us to stay on the route.

Keep running the race.

There will be times that our fleshly bodies will need refreshment and reviving. Along this marathon will be those places where there will be "Living Water" for our thirst, spiritual food in the Word, and often fruit of the spirit that we have cultivated for heart and soul health.

Keep running the race.

This is most important. As believers we must run for the duration of our life. At times we will get stuck, we will shed tears, we will get weary or listen to the voice of "the cheater" (Satan). However, one thing is for certain—There Are No Shortcuts.

Keep running the race

When you arrive at the "finish line" you will win
the crown of the Kingdom.

—Cathi Rumbaugh

Little Guys

"People were bringing little children to Jesus for him to place
his hands on them, but the disciples rebuked them. When Jesus
saw this, he was indignant. He said to them, 'Let the little
children come to me, and do not hinder them, for the kingdom
of God belongs to such as these.'" (Mark 10:13-14 NIV)

"Miss E-Tah, Miss E-Tah, can I start the "Butterfly Prayer?" It was an excited request from one of the three-year olds in my class of three to five year olds. (He has his very own special loving way of pronouncing my name.)

For several months, we had been using the "Butterfly Prayer" along with hand motions or butterfly puppets in Little Kidz Church as preparation for our opening prayer. By the time we finish reciting the little ditty, the children have settled down and are ready to pray to our heavenly Father. The poem gets their attention and they are able to focus. I was pleasantly surprised that this little guy was so eager to lead the poem. I began to think of the many times when I've wondered if the children understand what is being taught in class. Are they really learning about Jesus or is this just "play time" for them? The Holy Spirit quickly prompted me to the truth in the Scripture, Proverbs 22:6, which admonishes parents to "start children off on the way they should go." After prayer, we continued with singing praise songs, our lesson on Zacchaeus, and a craft to reinforce the lesson. As a review, I asked if anyone could tell me the story of Zacchaeus. I was planning to retell it for additional emphasis. I looked around the room and unexpectedly saw a little four-year old visitor with her hand raised. I called on her and she began to tell the story as only a small child can. Now, I was really excited!

For the second time that morning, God demonstrated to me that these little ones were really learning about Him. I was so pleased and thankful that God exhibited the results of teaching these "little guys" every Sunday morning. Although I have always known the importance of children knowing Jesus as soon as they have understanding—that truth was abundantly confirmed to me that day. I then fully understood why Jesus said, "Let the little children come to me, and do not hinder them, for the kingdom of God belongs to such as these (v. 14)."

What a gentle reminder that everything we do unto the Lord for children has eternal consequences.

—Juanita Adamson

Look at Me

"But whoso hearkeneth unto me shall dwell safely, and shall
be quiet from the fear of evil." (Proverbs 1:33 KJV)

Many of us have been privileged to live during what has become known
as "A Phenomenal Century (1911-2011). We've witnessed: The Wright
Brothers first flight (1911); the moon-landing mission (1969); and the
Mars rover expeditions (2003–present). In addition to the Titanic
disaster (1912) and two world wars (1914–1918 and 1939–1945), we have
experienced Pearl Harbor (1941), Korea, Vietnam, Iraq, Afghanistan
and others—and the killing of Osama bin Laden (2011), whose mortally
wounded body was openly displayed like meat in a market.

Added to these historic events are the isolation of the DNA, cloning,
laser surgeries, in-door plumbing, microwave ovens (1947), pizzas, and
Happy Meals—just to name a few of the events where man at times
seems to say to God, "LOOK AT US." China has also lifted up the
world's largest Ferris wheel (2008), with Singapore following with a sky
park that boasts of a ship structured to span the top of two skyscrapers
(over 656 feet high). Even the World Trade Center, destroyed in 2001,
has boldly been rebuilt with words of defiance directed at our enemies.

With the sincerest conviction, I believe that the God of the
universe—the Creator of all things—is warning us with His own
declaration, "LOOK AT ME." In one instance, man's "indestructible"
ship, the Titanic, had a horrific meeting with God's indestructible
iceberg. Also, the entire world is experiencing what have become known
as "historic" natural disasters. These events, along with other prideful
acts of men, should cause us all to "Look at God"— the only source
of our safety and freedom from fear, and our only hope for eternal life.

—Phyllis Andrews

My Heartfelt Thanks

"Delight yourself also in the Lord. And He shall give
you the desires of your heart." (Psalm 37:4 NKJV)

One Sunday morning during worship I felt the power of the Holy Spirit
in such a special way. When I opened my eyes, I saw our Pastor walk
over to a little boy who was being held by his mom. Pastor Jeff prayed
over the boy, and seemingly, his heart was always in sync with Jesus'
healing power:

> "Is anyone among you sick? Let him call for the elders of
> the church, and let them pray over him, anointing him with
> oil in the name of the Lord" (James 5:14 NKJV).

As part of the prayer ministry, I was called to the altar to pray for
people. I fixed my eyes on the excited mother carrying the little boy
to the altar. The rash he had was gone. God had used Pastor Jeff to
heal that little boy. I had never experienced God's healing power in
person. My heart was pounding as God covered me with the desire to
heal. I found a book on the healing power of God so I started to read
it—Thinking to myself "I will be ready to heal right when I finish it."

Thanksgiving morning (2014), my husband, Scott, and I were
getting prepared for dinner. My brother called saying Mom wasn't doing
well. She was in bed crying and shaking. He said she needed anxiety
medicine. As I hung up the phone I felt God urging me to go pray
over my mom. Upon arriving at my parent's house, I found my brother
ranting and raving. To this day I don't remember what he said. All I
know is that my mom needed me. Scott and I went into the bedroom
where we found both Dad and Mom. Dad was quite concerned for the
love of his life. Scott walked over to Mom's side of the bed and I sensed
God telling me to go to Dad's side. Scott started to pray with one hand
on Dad and one on Mom. Then God had me finish the prayer. I could
feel the Holy Spirit move into Mom's back—removing the anxiety and

depression from her body. I then heard Dad cry out "Thank you Lord, Praise you Lord." Never in my life had I heard him praise God from his heart.

My brother told me that I needed a new religion. I told him "I tried that once, but now I have a Great Physician who gave Mom the medicine she needed."

I found the healing book the other day with the book marker right where I had stopped reading it. Books are good, but the Maker of heaven and earth is the One who gives life.

—Sonya Andres

Dedicated to Pastor Jeff Etcheverry (March 22, 2013)

The Death Wish

"You belong to your father, the devil, and you want to
carry out your father's desires. He was a murderer from the
beginning, not holding to the truth, for there is no truth
in him. When he lies, he speaks his native language, for
he is a liar and the father of lies." (John 8:44 NIV)

I have always had ups and downs with depression. Sometimes I just take to my bed and sleep for days at a time. Other times I have entertained thoughts of dying—Most of the time they have been just fleeting thoughts and never a real desire to die. However, there was a time when I really did not feel it was worthwhile to live—What for? My life had no meaning. I was a mother, daughter, sister and a wife, but I saw no meaning, no love, not anything. My feelings were bad enough that I confided in my OB-GYN doctor who referred me to a psychiatrist. I made an appointment, but would have to wait a week—"I could put my pending death on hold for a week."

I was nervous the day of the appointment. A week to wait seemed forever. I walked up to the desk and stated my name and appointment time. The receptionist looked confused. She said there was no appointment for me. "No appointment, after I had nervously waited a week. What would I do now?" She said I could reschedule or they could work me in. I could not believe that no one cared enough to understand that I wanted to die! I told her to "forget it," and in tears I turned and walked out the door and to my car, where I sat and cried my heart out. I did not know what to do! However, when the tears finally stopped, calm came over me and I felt a renewed strength. "I would pull myself up by the boot straps and be something. I didn't need anyone to love me. I could be strong. I would be someone my family could be proud of." I believe God intervened that day—making me realize that the only love I needed was His. The only strength I needed was His. So, the two of us walked away together that day; me leaning on Him and Him supporting me in my weakness.

—Sue Walker

The Lord Spoke

"Ye are the salt of the earth:" (Matthew 5:13 KJV)

Amazingly, I believe that I've heard the Lord speak clearly, personally to me three times through the power of His Holy Spirit. How do I know it was God, you ask?

- Each time He spoke a direct answer to my question.
- Although His answer was a reprimand, it was never an attack. His direction was firm and loving.
- His words were obviously NOT ones I would have chosen for myself.

With those guidelines in place, come with me on one such occasion back in October 1986:

I had lived in Memphis, Tennessee, from birth until October 1st of that year and our family had just been transferred by Delta Airlines to live and work in the greater Cincinnati, Ohio, area.

We found a lovely home and straight away I was regularly on call to teach at the local high school. I began to learn the ins and outs of leaving a southern town and what to expect after living in a town just across from the Mason Dixon line. The folks were friendly. The students in most cases were respectful, but one thing was so hurtful to me that it was painful. I prayed and prayed, but the more it continued the more devastated I became.

"What on earth could be that bad," you ask? I had my Lord, my health, my family, a home, a job, a church, and friends. What could be missing? I'll explain. In the forty-two years I had lived in Memphis, I had not heard the Lord's name taken in vain in my presence. You're right. That's what I said. Profanity was just not a common occurrence. I had been brought up in the church way of life. Everything my family and I did involved Christian friends and activities. People on the street did not curse in public, especially not in a lady's presence—at least not back then. Maybe the Lord had kept me in a cocoon that far, but when we moved He had an even bigger lesson to teach me:

I was driving home from teaching school one afternoon. I had prayed, pled and cried out to God. It hurt so much. Every day I would hear the students in the hallways, the teachers in their lounge, and people on the streets cursing the names of Jesus. I was at my wit's end. "Father," I cried in desperation, "What can I do?" I believe God answered - "Jane, you hear My Name from their lips more than they hear My Name from yours."

"Wow, Lord!" What a revelation that was to me.

I began learning the students' names and taking an interest in their lives. The Lord gave me many opportunities to speak His Name in love to folks around me.

> Too often are we so preoccupied with our own hurt feelings that we fail to be God's salt in the earth—the mineral that adds flavor.

"Ye are the salt of the earth..."

—Jane Hatfield

The Meet-And-Greet

"But as touching brotherly love ye need not that I
write unto you: for ye yourselves are taught of God to
love one another." (1 Thessalonians 4:9 KJV)

Meet-and-Greet events are traditionally planned to provide opportunities for like-minded people to get to know one another, to engage in casual conversation, to sometimes exchange business cards, and often to reminisce with those you haven't seen in a long time.

I recently went to the funeral of a wonderful older friend. She and I had shared many silly moments of laughter about life and what a wonderful sense of humor our Lord has. Interestingly, her home-going service was "Skyped" to those who for one reason or another were unable to attend. As I sat there, I mused on how this electronic age is sadly depriving us of those important hugs and shared salty tears that are the glue that bind us together. They help us to communicate heart-to-heart in the joys and sadness of grief, but "Where has the family gone?" Where are those faces that remind us of our heritage; those faces that say "oh how much she looks like Grandma or Aunt Jo; 'wow,' that silver streak is just like Grandpa's hair was before he died?"

Some people texted their condolences, some tweeted, and some "liked" the sympathy section on Facebook and added their names to the blogs of other mourners. What I saw as missing was that warm embrace or handshake with other human beings. There have been other times when we have eaten at one local restaurant that we have seen elderly people who seem to migrate there just for the waitress to smile and ask how their day is going. To ask if they "want the same thing" to eat or drink because they have taken the time to get to know that person over the years. We can sometimes become impatient with the old gentleman who takes too much time at the post office counter because he enjoys having friendly conversation with the clerk. On one recent occasion to go there, I was so happy to see how the postal clerk spoke softly and patiently, even repeating her instructions several times until an aged man understood what he was to do with a returned package.

Please, let's not let this electronic age and our "so-called-important" busyness rob us of the fellowships that God intended. Our senses of humor and our overwhelming need for companionship were given to us by our Creator. So if He can smile and bring joy to others through us, what a different world this could be. Try saying "Good Morning" to a stranger sometimes. You'll probably scare him to death, but he will remember your kindness the rest of the day.

Family, fellowship, and friendship are "touching and agreeing" kinds of sports. They are great fun and can be virtually painless.

—Phyllis Andrews

The Small Things

"For whoever has despised the day of small things
shall rejoice..." (Zechariah 4:10 ESV)

I gratefully retired over twenty years ago from what I thought was an important, self-assuring, civil service position in a major bustling city. However, on one day recently I found myself fussing and fuming in frustration with what I considered as the same mundane activities every morning of every day: Wake up, make the bed, and stop at the bathroom before going from room to room opening the window blinds—each in its own specific slant to either control the sunlight or the eyes of the neighborhood. *In our other house in another state all of the blinds could be wide open because we lived on almost six acres of land, etc., etc., etc.* – [*italics* added in an attempt to maximize your vision of my pity-party that continued.] "I do the same thing every day, Lord. Is this what the rest of life is going to be about?"

Days later—and after apologizing to *"Abba"* [Father God] for my childish [internal] hissy-fit—I followed the same morning routine, but when I got to the "room-to-room-blind-opening part" my self-centeredness became a time of rejoicing. As I arrived at each window, I became aware of specific blessings in each deliberate motion I made. As the blinds in the great room parted, I rejoiced at seeing the mountain peaks with their snow covering. The birds were going from branch to branch seemingly happy within their little communities. The bedroom window provided light on the blessing of my new bedspread with its purple and green embroidery. It also gave me a glimpse of the prosperity and health of my neighbors and their families. The cat came out of hiding and greeted me gratefully without a care in the world. I heard the furnace come on as it provided heat to the house, and then the telephone rang, signaling a pleasant caller on the other end of the line.

It's all about how you choose to look at things in life. When we learn to cherish "the small things," God causes us to rejoice in all things.

What Joy - What Revelation - What Peace - What Grace!

—Phyllis Andrews

The Valleys Called "Why?" or "Why Me?"

"Blessed is the man who perseveres under trial, because
when he has stood the test, he will receive the crown of
life that God has promised to those who love him."
(James 1:12 NIV)

What is inside our inner self comes out in our "Why?" or "Why me?" moments when life seems to redirect our paths. It is hard not to get angry, lose our temper, or turn to despair. Instead, we should pause, pray, and let the Holy Spirit calm us. Whether we feel like it or not, we need to "Praise God" and declare a miracle in our time of uncertainty. He will bring us out of our valley when we exercise our faith. A scripture that helps me when I don't see the light at the end of the tunnel is, "I can do all things through Christ who strengthens me (1 Corinthians 10:13, NIV)."

When I am lost in a valley, I feel the need to love or forgive when I do not want to. It is hard to do, but I must—through persistent prayer—exercise those emotions in order to find peace. Then, I can move through the circumstances of the valley I am in. When it is time to fight the battle, with God's help, I receive His blessings. The scenario of the battle, as I look back, shows me how I was blessed. He turned my scars to stars! Joy does come after my mourning! Patience is a virtue! It's what I call "Getting through the going-through stage."

Always remember God when you are in a valley. He's always right beside you; you are never alone. He will never leave you. Call on Him; exercise your faith by putting it into action—"For we live by faith, not by sight (2 Corinthians 5:7 NIV)." You will then be able to climb up out of your valley as He leads you. Later, a time will come when you will share the story of your valley. It will become your personal testimony, as well as a blessing to someone going through a similar valley at an appointed time. Remember, God works in mysterious ways; His wonders to perform.

We have a tendency to forget just how big God is. He is bigger than our valleys! Declare His goodness! Put your faith and hope in Him! Talk to Him! Praise Him! There will be a revival!

—Lynne Brown

Top of the World

*"My steps have held to your paths; my feet have
not stumbled." (Psalm 17:5 NIV)*

The trail starts at an old weathered and splintered fence, and has few obstacles to trip the trekker. To the bench sitter, the route appears level and easy, but for the hiker the way quickly rises in the brush near the foothills. The moderate incline grows steadily steeper with large rocks that seem to appear mysteriously, causing the unsuspecting to stumble. The leisurely walk quickly becomes precarious. A cool drink of water is necessary as less experienced walkers decide whether to continue. Many return to the bench. The seasoned hiker goes on, knowing the reward of reaching the top. Longer breaks become essential. Perhaps a prayer is breathed as the ascent grows more challenging. The hiker endures the unstable climb; the top is only a few steps away. Then suddenly, the pinnacle appears within reach and a final thrust to the summit is crucial. Exhilarated, the hiker revels in the view from what seems the top of the world.

Frequently, God calls us to His work. It might be as insignificant as dumping trash or as exciting as a ministry impacting many. But often—instead of answering God's call we become bench sitters—shutting out His voice and using our fears and busy lives as excuses not to obey. Other times, we start with great gusto, but like the inexperienced hiker we are totally unprepared. As we trust in our own strength and wisdom, fatigue and discouragement overcome us and we quit. There are also times we have prepared like the most experienced hiker readies to scale a mountain. We hear God's voice and check that our motives are sincere and pure. We pray and wait for His direction to guide our steps and confront the terrain—the challenges and disappointments. Then our willingness, obedience and preparation are rewarded in God's victorious finish—our top of the world experience.

—Juanita Adamson

You're Not Done Yet!

"Even when I am old and gray, do not forsake me, my
God, till I declare your power to the next generation, your
mighty acts to all who are to come." (Psalm 71:18 NIV)

One especially exasperating, warm Wednesday night my thoughts, like hundreds of loose marbles, began to roll and jolt in my exhausted mind—"you're too old for this. Just tell the pastors, you're done! It's too much stress!" Feelings continued to gush uncontrollably. "If it's not problems with the kids, it's getting leaders to work with these unruly street urchins. Besides, no one cares, so why should I?" Talk about discouragement at its best— or is it at its worst?

The closer I got home the more persuasive the arguments became. The idea of quitting spread like an uncontainable forest fire. Excitedly, I began to practice my defense verbally as if someone was listening: "I have things to do on Wednesday nights just like everyone else! Besides, I'm tired of subjecting myself to abuse from sassy kids! They're not learning anything anyway."

At the stop light, the Holy Spirit alerted me to the danger of my thoughts. I immediately prayed a simple prayer, "help me, Jesus" to quiet my mind. As I reached home, I quickly drove up the driveway and turned off the ignition. In the dark solitude of my car, the Holy Spirit reminded me of a time many years ago when I felt totally inadequate and ineffectual. I recalled I was home from work because of illness when He dealt with me regarding teaching Wednesday night classes for young girls, especially those children who are unchurched. I believe that God said that if they learned anything, it should be how much He loves them. I could not deny the heart-to-heart, ending weeks of turmoil and indecision for me.

As I sat quietly, I sensed God saying, "I will let you know when you're too old or are done with what I have given you to do." That summer night, I learned:

- First, **God will never forsake us**. He is the one, who measures the success of what He has given us to do—using His measurement. He never compares us to others and what He has given them to do. Success is often not visible to us.

- Second, **even if we are old and gray**, we must continue to "declare [His] power to the next generation, [His] mighty acts to all who are to come (v. 18)."
- Third, **we're not done until He says we're done**.

—Juanita Adamson

Walls

"By faith the walls of Jericho fell down, after they were compassed about seven days." (Hebrews 11:30 KJV)

"It feels just like I have a stone wall lodged in my heart," I complained to my friend as she gently attempted to explain the Gospel of Jesus Christ to me. "I just don't get it," I continued feeling more and more frustrated. My friend, after several valiant attempts, finally ceased her efforts to gently counsel me that children of God are taught to shake the dust from their feet and move on if your attempt to present the Word of God is not accepted. I remained silent, confused and with a very heavy heart. Depression enveloped me like a heavy shroud.

> "He [Satan]hath blinded their eyes, and hardened their hearts; that they should not see with their eyes, nor understand with their heart, and be converted, and I should heal them" (John 12:40 KJV).

But wait! Unbeknownst to me a tiny seed had been miraculously planted in my hardened heart by my persistent friend!

Decades passed. Other Christians witnessed to me about the saving grace of Jesus Christ. That tiny seed of faith—smaller even than a mustard seed—began to grow. I began to seek Jesus Christ for myself. It was and is not an easy or a quick journey. My hardened heart was resilient and rebellious—uncannily alike the Israelites described in the Old and New Testaments. At first, only a minuscule crevice opened up in that stony edifice within my heart. Then a larger more obstinate stone was pried loose, muttering and complaining. I think that stone was called "a woman's right to choose," replaced by a conviction that "right to life" was God's truth. Other stones followed the first. Some fell with ease, but some required the assistance of a two-by-four wielded by God's own hand! The stone requiring the two-by-four was called "living together before marriage." The result of the two-by-four was an immediate marriage. Then another stone fell. It was labeled "homosexuality is acceptable." According to God's Word, homosexuality is a sin (see Leviticus 18:22, KJV). A softened and humbled heart began to be revealed in me. This process of sanctification is a continual work in progress.

"Wow," I say to myself today, "This feeling is almost beyond description." A sense of well-being suffuses my soul. There is a sensation of warmth and flexibility flooding through my formerly cold and frigid heart. Joy and peace have become my constant companions. Depression has taken flight and no longer stretches out its icy fingers to haunt me. I walk by faith. There is love in my heart for humanity even if I may not like some of them very much—"Love the sinner, but hate the sin," is a good adage to live by.

"By faith my walls of Jericho tumbled down."

I thank God for the many Christians who kept the faith and witnessed to me, even in the face of my rebellious and hardened heart.

Do you have a hardened heart?
Seek the Lord with an open mind and you
will find Him as He has promised.

—Catherine Ricks Urbalejo

Wrestling With God

"So Jacob was left alone, and a man wrestled with him till daybreak.
When the man saw that he could not overpower him, he touched
the socket of Jacob's hip so that his hip was wrenched as he wrestled
with the man. Then the man said, "Let me go, for it is daybreak."
But Jacob replied, "I will not let you go unless you bless me." The
man asked him, "What is your name?" "Jacob," he answered.
Then the man said, "Your name will no longer be Jacob, but Israel
because you have struggled with God and with humans and have
overcome. Jacob said, "Please tell me your name." But he replied,
"Why do you ask my name?" Then he blessed him there."
(Genesis 32:24–30 NIV)

This well-known biblical story has always fascinated me. Why would
Jacob wrestle with God all night? On the surface that seems rather
impertinent. Then why would God put Jacob's hip out of joint? Even
after being struck (v. 25), why would Jacob still not let his grip on "the
Man" go until He had blessed him? Why did Jacob get a new name? Of
course I do not know the answers to those questions so you will have
to discern for yourself if my thoughts on this biblical story resonate
with you or not.

At the time of this episode, Jacob was a very frightened man. He
was alone and fearing that his brother Esau would kill him in retaliation
for his deceitful act of stealing his brother's birthright.

As we walk the trail to the Throne of Grace, our daily struggles,
whatever they might be, mirror Jacob's difficulties. We may be coming
with a past array of sinful baggage like Jacob or as believers, bedeviled
by the problems of everyday life. What did Jacob do? He would not let
go— He persevered all night and he endured. However, for his efforts
Jacob received a painful limp for the rest of his life. So what was the
point of putting Jacob's hip out of joint? Perhaps this would serve as a
constant reminder to him that he had struggled with God and endured;
a type of "thorn in the flesh" analogous to that which Paul the apostle

endured (see 2 Corinthians 12:7-9). God reminded Paul that His grace was sufficient even in the presence of this affliction.

At daybreak, after a night of struggle with Jacob, God honored his request for a blessing and gave him something in addition to the dislocated hip. He gave him a new name. That name was "Israel" meaning "one who prevails with God". Perhaps Jacob, now *Israel*, had a new heart as a result of his struggle. I think this must indeed be so. In heaven we too will be given a new name after we have completed our final struggles on earth (see Revelation 2:17 as an example)! That caused me to ponder exactly what receiving a blessing from God really means? Blessings are a central tenant of God's purpose for humanity.[5] There appear to be two accepted ideas that embody the concept of a blessing.[5] One is the state of being in a favored status with God. The other is receipt of God-given power to walk in prosperity and success through life's circumstances.

No wonder Jacob held on until God blessed him—
And so must we!

—Catherine Ricks Urbalejo

[5] http://www.biblestudytools.com/dictionary/blessing/

~ Section 3 ~
SUFFICIENT GRACE

"And he said unto me, My grace is sufficient for thee:
for my strength is made perfect in weakness…"

(2 Corinthians 12:9 KJV)

A Calculating Mind

"Why wasn't this perfume sold and the money given to the
poor? It was worth a year's wages." (John 12:5 NIV)

When I first left home, I was not a Christian and therefore difficult
finances were part of the "wages of sin" that I endured. We never
had enough money for anything. If I worked an extra shift, the
man I lived with (who is now my husband) called in sick to work.
If I set aside money for bills, something broke or the electric bill
doubled or the money was stolen. Something always came to take
away our profit.

When the Bible says that those who trust in the Lord will never be
seen begging for bread, I suppose the opposite is true as well. On more
than one occasion, I filled grocery bags at my mother's home, and if we
did not have a program called "WIC" or women, infants, and children,
we would have gone hungry after our daughter was born-- even though
we both worked full time in the restaurant industry. When I did the
math, we should have been okay. Not wealthy by any stretch of the
imagination, but okay. Reality was different. Reality does not obey the
rules of math.

Poverty, hard work, and hopelessness experienced day after day,
month after month, and year after year, leads to a calculating mind.
Everything costs something. And that something was always more
than what I had to give. Every joy was chased closely behind with
what I might call a wasting sorrow. It made me suspicious of every
good thing.

There was good reason for that. When I chose to live in sin, God
did not bring his blessings into my life. It was not because He didn't
love me. It was because my sin left me unprotected and open to attacks
from Satan. It was my choice to refuse to serve God, but I paid dearly
for it in more ways than words will ever be able to capture. When Satan
is your master, death is like a poison that permeates every good thing,
gradually turning what is light into darkness.

I remember the day I gave my heart to Christ. When I sat in my living room the next day, the sun shone in and I remember it as a light inside a tomb. That's how low I was. Yet I was not out of the woods spiritually until I got married. Until then, I was still living in sin, even as a new Christian. God worked to heal me, but I was still open to attack because of my sin. I remember clearly that once I was married, I literally heard a door swing to close. The attacks—mental, spiritual, physical, and financial—were now going to be greatly hindered because I had entered into God's protection. Yet I continued to live with a calculating mind. It is the fruit of sin.

When I gave anything to anyone, I counted the cost. Like Judas, I could not see any value in waste, no matter the expression of love embedded in the sacrifice. When I received, I counted the cost. I measured my value in numbers. As our lives began to improve for the first time, I calculated every financial move. We lived in a decent home for the first time in the five years we had been together. We had food every week to put on the table. I was able to clothe my daughter with some new things, not just other people's left overs. God moved the burden of overwhelming work out of my life, allowing me more time with my daughter. Healing was slow but steady. Even so, I did not trust anything. It was a long time before I was able to see a blessing without feeling a great sense of apprehension about how much it would cost me.

My young daughter is now a young woman. She is twenty years old and I am trying to teach her what I know about budgeting, but I catch myself using a calculating mind at times. I want to bless her, but I sometimes do so in carefully measured ways. When we look at her resources and what she might give to others, I am finding it difficult to explain what is to be counted carefully and what is to be given in a spirit of joy. I want to be sure we have enough; I want to be sure she has enough as she goes out on her own. I also want to give to God, and I want to do it cheerfully. Yet my calculating mind is hard to silence. It is my personal struggle with faith.

A calculating mind fails to see the grace in giving. A calculating mind does not really believe God will honor our sacrifices and will make provision. A calculating mind does the math and ignores the times in the past when God blessed us. A calculating mind holds onto money and possessions, hoarding what should be given. A calculating mind retains resentment when the gifts one receives aren't quite right. It is a mind full of fear, full of selfishness, and full of bitterness. It is the opposite of all that Christ was and is. It is not the fruit of the spirit.

Is it good to be frugal? Yes. Christ was never wasteful. He took up the leftovers after his miracle of the fishes and the loaves (see Matthew 14:19-21). Yet we are to live in a spirit of faith, not fear. We are to be generous, lending freely, and we are to be joyful, not bitter. I find it easiest to give to those who are good to me, but this is also the fruit of a calculating mind. We are to love our enemies. Even, and probably especially, when it costs us something.

When we are tempted to focus on counting the cost and when we can't see the beauty of the sacrifice, we need to remember that it was Judas who embraced a calculating mind and that it was Christ who valued the sacrifice of love. Who do we want to be like? As for me, I am reminded daily that I must choose to try to grow ever more like Christ.

—Kristen Welch

Accept Your Healing

"For I will restore health unto thee, and I will heal thee of
thy wounds, saith the Lord." (Jeremiah 30:17 KJV)

Recently I became ill and when I don't feel good I tend to become depressed. That was my illness—depression. God does not want us ill, so I turned to my faith to help me through. He gave me strength through the above verse from the Word of God, the Holy Bible—How powerful is that?

God wants you well! He wants you healthy and strong in every single area of your life. He wants you to be spiritually strong:

- Strong in faith; Strong in the Word; Strong in His love: He wants you to be well in your minds -- to be strong and stable emotionally. He wants you to have a healthy will; a will that's aligned with His will. He wants your body to be well. He wants you free from the bondages of pain, sickness, and care. Free from the worries and woes of this earthly life.

Your heavenly Father wants you well! What's more, in this day and hour, He *needs* you well:

- He needs you living in victory and healing so that you can teach others how to do it too. We're living in a time when that kind of knowledge is an absolute necessity. There's no more time for the Body of Christ (those who have accepted Jesus Christ as their Lord and Savior) to limp along, uninformed and unprepared for the devil's attacks.

In fact, here is what I believe the Lord has "said" to me: "The further you go, the more dangerous things in the earth will become. People will have to grow in the realities of knowing that their sins are forgiven through Jesus Christ our Lord—In also knowing the "how-to's" of living by faith in order to live in the great and overcoming way I have planned for them."

God wants us to be healthy and strong as witnesses in these last days to a world that's filled with terror—witnesses of His love, His grace and His power.

Be reminded that: "He sent His word, and healed them, and delivered them from their destruction" (Psalm 107:20, KJV).

—Tancy Elliott

Babble, Babble, Toil and Trouble!

"Incline your ear, and come unto me: hear, and your soul
shall live; and I will make an everlasting covenant with you,
even the sure mercies of David." (Isaiah 55:3 KJV)

Today I had an epiphany! It all started in a strange way. I was listening with interest to an evangelical speaker on the usual local Christian radio channel as I drove to town for my daily exercise class. Suddenly the station began to broadcast two independent programs with individual speakers simultaneously. A babble of incoherent and incomprehensible sound emerged as the new speaker crashed into the original broadcast with equal volume. I was annoyed, yet sufficiently interested in the original speaker to make an effort to hear him through the din. What was fascinating to me was that at one level my brain received the collective duo of voices as babble. However, if I made an extreme effort to focus my brain I could choose to identify and isolate the original speaker from the collective muddle of voices. I was able to tune the other speaker out. The result—I could distinguish the desired speaker clear as a bell with the other speaker's voice retreating into the background as a mildly irritating hum. I continued to listen to the original program with pleasure.

It struck me that this incident was a metaphor for a believer's life. The world calls loudly in a babble of discordant and strident voices, rudely intruding into our lives and sometimes making us collectively deaf to God's still clear and quiet voice. I was thrilled that I was quite capable of choosing to "tune out" the discordant babble and listen to the one voice. In the same way, we can choose to hear God's voice above the noise, confusion, toil, and trouble of the world we live in. We must be willing to make the effort not only to choose Jesus as our Lord and Savior, but also to choose to hear God's still quiet voice as we go about the daily challenges of life in this clamorous world? What critical—but very relevant—choices these can be.

—Catherine Ricks Urbalejo

Burden of My Soul

"So Jesus said to them, Because of your unbelief, for assuredly, I say to you, if you have faith as a mustard seed, you will say to this mountain, 'Move from here to there,' and it will move and nothing will be impossible for you." (Matthew 17:20 NKJV)

Each grain of sand in this small bag that I hold represents a small portion of burdens that my soul has carried, is carrying—or if I choose—will carry. We have a God who has sufficient grace to dissolve all these burdens. In my mind, this pile of sand has formed a desert-like mountain of sorrows, distress, pain, rebellion, and other sins. The mountain that the enemy has placed before my eyes cannot be moved by my good deeds, but it can be moved by diligent and fervent prayers to my heavenly Father. In Luke 1:37, the Bible says that "For with God nothing will be impossible."

As I take on these burdens, I see that I'm undone and barren. God is preparing me to be strong enough to move the mountain so it can be sowed with God's love and His Word. It can be planted with God's seed and the process of growth can begin. God's "living water" is fertilizing the seeds with kindness and love. The fruit will start maturing for harvest. God gives us the strength and courage not to be defeated or grow weary from the adversities.

As I count my blessings, I share them with God's children, especially those who are lost and need to be introduced to the love of Jesus. As each of these souls becomes intertwined with my life, these relationships take root in God's vineyard.

The mountain that began as desolate sand is now rich with the fruit of love and life. The harvest is lush and more abundant than one can image. "Lord, I present this harvest for inspection and desire to hear you say, "Well done, my good and faithful servant."

—Cathi Rumbaugh

Choices

"Those who know your name will trust in you, for you, LORD,
have never forsaken those who seek you." (Psalm 9:10 KJV)

How quickly December arrived! It seemed as though we had just finished performing our annual out-door drama, "Walk Thru Bethlehem," and it was that time again. The many details to prepare for this presentation of the Nativity for our community rushed in like a tsunami. As the performance dates drew closer, it was apparent that we weren't ready. It was difficult not to get discouraged and to give up. And even more of a challenge to reassure the individuals faithfully attending rehearsals that we were going to really make it.

We offered a simple prayer before the rehearsals even began: "Lord, this presentation is all yours not mine, you take care of it." I refused to become disheartened. However, not immune to Satan's fiery darts, thoughts of failure continued to niggle in my mind. Presenting something not worthy of our Lord was totally unacceptable. Perhaps it was only my pride or my desire to please the King of Kings; I wasn't quite sure. I searched my heart to ensure I had the right motive. I believe that God, in His awesome faithfulness, relieved the nagging anxiety I was feeling. I felt him say, "It's going to be alright, you'll see." Yes, I could see; it was a test of faith in God. But was I up for the test? My choices were simple. I could either quit (the easy way out) or continue and trust my heavenly Father for the finished product. I chose to trust and the performances went on. God was not only glorified, but He was very much in control of its outcome.

Daily, I remind myself that God has promised to never leave me or forsake me, no matter how serious or insignificant my situations may be. I must be mindful that if it concerns me, it concerns my heavenly Father, because He loves me just as He loves you.

But, a strange phenomenon occasionally occurs—I fall prey to that old habit of worrying about a situation instead of immediately trusting God for the results. However, after the dust settles, I recognize that it would have been much less stressful to trust in my heavenly Father from the "get go." He not only knows exactly what is needed, but foresees the future.

Hopefully, you see that you and I are on a journey; learning as we go. And God—He is the patient and loving teacher.

—Juanita Adamson

Getting Old is For The Birds

"Even to your old age I am He, and to gray hairs I
will carry you. I have made, and I will bear; I will
carry and will save." (Isaiah 46:4 ESV)

Lunch in a nursing home is a trip.
Imagine 70 people at various tables.
40 of them have no idea why they're here. 10 know why they're
here, but they're upset because not all attention is on them. 15
are wondering where their spouse is. 5 are trying to figure out
how to change the TV channel.... with their cell phone.
All 70 want to go to the bathroom. NOW.
35 people are too hot, 35 are too cold, and the staff
is roasting. "Who keeps opening that door?"
68 want coffee, only 9 actually drink coffee,
"More creamer, please!"
58 want soup, 12 want salad. 5 people will actually
eat soup, 53 will wonder what's in the bowl.
The food arrives: 35 people ordered beef stew,
35 ordered grilled cheese.
"What's this? I didn't order this!" 68 people
thought they ordered oatmeal.
After dessert, 68 people say, "Don't I get dessert?"
"You already ate dessert."
"No, I didn't get any!"
Now it's over.
"What's next?"
60 people want to know what's for lunch, 40 have no
idea where they are, and there are still the upset 10. Oh
yeah, and 68 people have to go to the bathroom.

--

Though written humorously, the circumstances of aging can be a frightening and chaotic time. However, God's promise in it all is "I will carry, I will bear, I will save."

God's eternal arms never weaken—His vigilant protection never fails. We are His; He will not let go. He will bear you up, carry you on in your way, and carry you home at last. What a wonderful Savior!

—Sharon Byrd

God Is Good

"Yea, though I walk through the valley of the shadow of
death, I will fear no evil: for thou art with me; thy rod
and thy staff they comfort me." (Psalm 23:4 KJV)

Words to a familiar song flowed out of the home where we attend a
Friday night small group. We were late and they were in the midst of
worship—singing "God is Good All the Time"[6] —when we arrived.
Immediately, I was transported back in time prior to my dad's death.
He had been hospitalized for weeks before his doctor determined that
nothing more could be done medically. He was to be placed in long-
term care or sent home. My mother chose to take him home, but she
needed help providing care. This meant a change in our work schedules
and moving in with them temporarily.

I started work at 5:30 a.m., so I left the house at 4:30 to drive the
approximate thirty miles. During the trip, I listened to "God is Good
All the Time," repeatedly. We had received the song on a cassette the
month prior. The only problem was we had requested all future orders
to be in CD format since we were transitioning from cassettes. I was
annoyed at the company's inefficiency and intended on returning it.
However, I never had time to mail it back so the cassette sat unopened
until I began driving back and forth to work alone. It was a good thing
since the car I drove only had a cassette player. Listening to the song
became a comfort as I was indeed experiencing the "darkest night" and
needed "His light to shine." The lyrics became my companion and my
prayer, as I watched my dad's life ebb away. As I prayed and meditated
while on the road, the Holy Spirit assured me that as my beloved dad
"walked through the valley of the shadow of death," he would not be
afraid and he would not be alone. I found solace in the assurance that
my dad's new home would be heaven. He had given his heart to Jesus

---

[6] Moen, Don (1998 album God is Good-Worship with Don Moen); https://
en.m.wikipedia.org/wiki/God_Is_Good_-Worship_with_Don_Moen.

shortly before becoming ill and anxiously looked forward to going to his heavenly home.

Nineteen years have passed and I still remember feeling the presence of Jesus in the hospital room, in my parent's home, in the car, and especially with my dad as he transitioned to his forever home— God's light was shining brightly. He promises to always be with us, even in the "valley of the shadow of death," and it is a promise we can trust, especially when we are experiencing our "darkest night."

—Juanita Adamson

God Provides

"The rabble with them began to crave other food,
and again the Israelites started wailing and said, "If
only we had meat to eat!" (Numbers 11:4 NIV)

"The Lord said to Moses: "Bring me seventy of Israel's elders
who are known to you as leaders and officials among the people.
Have them come to the tent of meeting that they may stand there
with you. I will come down and speak with you there, and I will
take some of the power of the Spirit that is on you and put it on
them. They will share the burden of the people with you so that
you will not have to carry it alone." (Numbers 11:16–17 NIV)

My daughter and her husband were notified suddenly by their landlord
that they would have to move from their rental home of nine years.
After unsuccessfully searching for a rental home that would fit within
their budget, they decided the best option would be for the two of them
to split up. My daughter would need to move home to live with us until
their financial circumstances could improve. In the meantime, her
husband decided to ask his boss for an increase in pay. Unfortunately,
this was not possible. However, his boss, recognizing there might be
a problem of some sort, asked what the issue might be. Upon learning
that my daughter would have to move in with her family he proposed
a possible solution—they could move to Georgia, and work in the
company office there. Since the cost of living was 60% less there, the
kids decided to accept this gracious offer. The problems were not over,
however! The kids had only three weeks to move and find a place to live.

With such short notice, they needed both financial support and
help with packing their household goods. Sadly, we could not help
them with either of these needs. While I was reading the Bible and
praying for them, God brought to my attention the verses in the Book
of Numbers described above. These verses describe how the Israelites
had left Egypt and how God had provided manna for them to eat. But

they remembered the great food in Egypt and started grumbling for meat to eat. God again granted their wish by providing quail for them to eat. Soon Moses, their leader, also had a great need for assistance in religious matters, as well as support in his position as a mediator in the affairs of the people. God's answer was to delegate seventy helpers from the people to help Moses.

The circumstances in these verses inspired me to pray and enlist others to join with me in prayer and sourcing help for their bleak situation. God gave me the idea to call one of my daughter's friends who organized a crew to help pack the last of the items from their home. Through friends and family God also provided the means for them to make the move to Georgia.

It was truly a miracle—God always provides in time.

—Millie Wasden

Is My Thumb On The Scale?

"...for God sees not as man sees, for man looks at the
outward appearance, but the Lord looks at the heart."
(1 Samuel 16:7 NASB)

For three years when I was growing up in the late 1940's, my parents owned and operated a neighborhood grocery store.

This was the end of an era. Less than one in three householders owned an automobile and virtually no house had a garage. Public transportation was usually several blocks away and the local grocer got stock from a wholesaler who branded the store. My parents' store was "Hatfield's Dot Food Store." My mother ran the front of the store and my dad was the butcher.

We lived in Dayton, Kentucky, a small town of 9,000 on the south side of the Ohio River across from Cincinnati, Ohio.

My parents were honest, serving a lower income neighborhood. We lived one block from the store. It was not uncommon for my dad to get a call or receive a knock at the door after the store had closed in the evening. It would be a neighbor who forgot to get a bag of sugar or a stick of butter. My dad would get dressed, go down to the store, and open for that one customer and let them pay the next time they were in to shop. Rain, snow or shine, he served his customers.

I was the only child of a loving marriage that lasted sixty-six years when my dad died in 2000. During the summer months, at ages six to nine, I was in and out of the store with my friends several times a day. That, of course, was before credit cards and many of the customers dealt in cash, not having a checking account. Many times, after my mother would ring up the bill for the items the customer had put on the counter, I would hear the customer say, "Put it on the cuff."

"Putting it on the cuff" meant that my mother and dad gave the buyer credit at no interest. Less than 50% ever paid off what they owed my parents. But my dad had a warm and funny sense of humor. When I asked my dad, later, if a family could make a living running a neighborhood grocery store, he would say, not very seriously, "Only if I put my thumb on the scale," meaning that when he weighed a customer's meat purchase, only if he added weight by putting his thumb on the scale, could he make any profit. My dad never did and he didn't make any profit, going out of business in just three years, still holding more than a year's income in uncollectible credit he had extended to the neighborhood families. My parents had integrity.

There are, however, many people who go through life with their thumbs on the scale. It may be only a few dollars here and there. It may be failing to show income or adding ghost expenses on the tax return; shorting the food servers on their tips; or selling a car that needs undisclosed work. As innocent as these little actions may seem to them, it is stealing. It lowers one's self esteem, because the perpetrator knows it is dishonest.

Every society since creation has had those in all occupations, games, transactions or personal relationships who put or keep their thumbs on the scale. The Bible tells us that God sees no difference in dishonesty, whether it is putting your thumb on the scale or coveting your neighbor's wife or house—Misuse of benefits or pointing a gun at the bank teller will be treated alike. All are sins worthy of condemnation—and we will be answering to God for them.

Just remember that He is watching all the time and knows our innermost thoughts.

—Jerry Hatfield

I Wait For The Lord

"I wait for the Lord, my soul waits, and in His
word I put my hope." (Psalm 130:5 NIV)

For five long years I planted. During that time, I earned a doctorate and raised two small children. After that, for five long years I brought in the harvest—publishing, leading, teaching, and raising those same two kids as I worked as an Assistant Professor. Yet as hard as it was to plant and to harvest, I find it's sometimes more difficult to manage the time of winter; it is a time of rest and replenishment.

Although I spent my first two years in Sierra Vista, Arizona, driving long miles from campus to campus to teach as an adjunct, it was still far less taxing than my work for the university. Without any research to do, without any administrative work, and without much in the way of teaching in terms of junior or senior level courses, I entered a season of winter.

I thought my season of winter was over when I began my full time job last fall. However, even though God has brought me into full-time work—and even though I labor for hours over my teaching plans and over the papers I grade—new challenges arrive with the new blessings, and I have to continue to manage this season of winter. I long for the time I'll have the resources to plant again, to begin new research projects, to engage in creative work like writing, sewing, and painting. But I can't seem to get anything started. It is winter.

Even though I prefer the time of planting and harvest, I am learning a lot in this time of winter. I have learned that in the winter, God can speak to me in ways I don't allow him to when I'm busy with planting my own projects. In the winter, I have time to count my blessings, to stay up late talking with my loved ones, to walk my dog "Daisy" in long, lazy laps around the neighborhood, to knead dough and to peel apples for pies, to listen to the birds calling out to each other in the early hours, to read poetry, to dream new dreams...

In the winter, God repairs what is broken.

In the winter, I have time to search His word.

In the winter, I can ponder advice from Christian friends, and I can respond to my parents' gentle guidance.

In the winter, I think of others and their challenges. I forget my own.

In the winter, I can dream new dreams. I can dream of another season, which I have not experienced in a long, long time. I can dream of spring.

—Kristen Welch

I Will Lift Up My Eyes

"I will lift up mine eyes unto the hills, from whence cometh
my help. My help cometh from the LORD, which made
heaven and earth. He will not suffer thy foot to be moved: he
that keepeth thee will not slumber. Behold, he that keepeth
Israel shall neither slumber nor sleep. The LORD is thy
keeper: the LORD is thy shade upon thy right hand. The
sun shall not smite thee by day, nor the moon by night. The
LORD shall preserve thee from all evil: he shall preserve
thy soul. The LORD shall preserve thy going out and thy
coming in from this time forth, and even for evermore."
(Psalm 121 KJV)

I gaze at mountains high-soaring above
crags that were crafted with infinite love;
a tectonic movement, a volcanic shove,
mountains that manifest Creator's love.

I lift up my eyes, I study the hills;
in turn I'm uplifted, it's better'n pills!
I lift up my heart, no battle of wills
as He says to me: Peace. Peace, be still.

"...I WILL lift up my eyes..."
I see this action as a conscious choice:
Yes, Lord, I will lift up my gaze, my mind and heart and soul.
I will look outside of myself; I will seek
something bigger than myself.
I will choose to move beyond human emotions to an act of
willpower and of worship.
I will respond to my Creator God, aware of, but looking
beyond, my human circumstances that I may share the divine
perspective that "...this light momentary affliction is preparing

for us an eternal weight of glory beyond all comparison...
as we look not to the things that are seen but to the things
that are unseen..." (2 Corinthians 4:17–18 ESV).

Yes, Lord, I WILL lift up my eyes...and worship you!

—David Smith

Jesus' Last Words From the Cross

"It is finished." (John 19: 30 NASB)

The Bible records that Jesus made seven utterances from the Cross. Teachers and writers, among others, describe these as "The Seven Last Words" and "The Seven Cries from the Cross."

1. "Father, forgive them; for they do not know what they are doing." (Luke 23: 34 NASB):

Forgiveness is what the Cross is all about. Jesus— the sinless and perfect sacrifice—forgave all sins; past, present and future for those who accept His undeserved gift.

2. "Truly I say to you, today, you shall be with Me in 'Paradise.'" (Luke 23: 43 NASB):

These words were uttered to the criminal hanging beside him. He rebuked his fellow convict for "hurling abuse" at Jesus and begged "remember me when You come in Your kingdom."

When Jesus granted his request, He made it immediate by saying "today," He, thus, confirmed the Parable of the Laborers in the Vineyard, "So the last shall be first, and the first last" (Matthew 20:16 NASB):

3. "Woman, behold, your son." Then looking at the Apostle John, He said, "Behold, your mother." (John 19: 26–27 NASB):

As Jesus addressed His mother, Mary, the Bible uses the lower case "son." He recognizes Mary as His earthly mother and pays her that respect. He accepts His earthly duty to care for His mother, and, therefore, passes that responsibility to John.

John, the youngest apostle, was the only one to live on to die of natural causes some seventy years later. Some say he cared for Mary all her life and they both, likely, died in Ephesus.

4. "My God, My God, why have You forsaken me?" (Matthew 27: 46–47; Mark 15: 34–36 (NASB):

As He had done many times before, Jesus quoted from Old Testament Scripture. In this case, He was repeating Psalm 22 that was written by David.

As David did when he wrote and prayed to God in his distress, he first expressed the distress, but later in verses 3–5 and 9–10, he reaffirmed his trust in God.

Jesus was in constant prayer and communication with His Father and likely was praying the entire Psalm, although only the first phrase was audible.

5. "I am thirsty." (John 19: 28 NASB):

When the soldiers put the sour wine on a hyssop branch and touched it to Jesus' lips, it was His last bitter taste of the sins heaped upon Him.

6. "It is finished." (John 19: 30 NASB):

He had accomplished all for which He had come to Earth. Jesus determined the moment and the method of His death. This was fully expressed in John 17:1–26 (NASB).

7. "Father, into Your hands I commit My spirit." (Luke 23: 46 NASB):

He was not killed by the Romans or the Jews. "He bowed His head and gave up His spirit."

The Cross was necessary to pay the price of sin. Jesus took on all of mankind's sin. Three days later, He defeated the devil and death by rising from the grave. It is that risen Savior who we worship.

—Jerry and Jane Hatfield

Leaving the Past Behind

"...but this one thing I do, forgetting those things which
are behind, and reaching forth unto those things which are
before, I press toward the mark for the prize of the high
calling of God in Christ Jesus." (Philippians 3:13–14 KJV)

Spiritual bumps and bruises—inner aches and pains that just don't seem to go away. Most of us know what it's like to suffer from them, but too few of us know just what to do about them.

We limp along, hoping somehow those hidden wounds will magically stop hurting. Thinking that maybe (with a little extra sleep or an extra helping of dessert) that nagging sense of depression will finally disappear. But does it ever happen that way? *No!* I know; I've been there. But thank God, I'm not there anymore. You see, over the past few years, I've faced some fierce spiritual battles. And I've found out those battles can leave you bruised and beaten up on the inside. Just as surely as a fistfight can leave you bruised and beaten up on the outside.

Throughout our lives all kinds of distractions and temptations—such as life's worries, riches and evil desires—threaten to choke off our commitment to the Lord. What is needed is a "forgetting what is behind," meaning the corrupt world and our old life of sin. The healing of a bruised and beaten spirit doesn't come easy. The passing of time often worsens this condition. The reason is this: Instead of putting painful failures behind us, we often dwell on them until those failures become more real to us than the promises of God. We focus on them until we become bogged down in depression; frozen in our tracks by the fear that if we go on we'll only fail again. Therefore, if depression has put you into a spiritual nosedive, all you have to do to break out of it is to get your eyes off the past and onto your future. Your future has been guaranteed by Christ Jesus through the exceedingly great and precious promises in His Word.

Chances are that won't come easily to you at first. Your mind has probably had years of practice in focusing on the past. Like an old horse that habitually heads for the barn in the evening, your negative thoughts will probably start galloping that direction every time you give them any slack. So, don't give them that slack. Keep the reigns tight. Purposely meditate on the Word of God [Read Philippians 3:12–21]. Diligently replace those thoughts of the past with scriptural promises about your future. Then, instead of being a wounded soldier, you'll become the conquering warrior God made you to be.

—Tancy Elliott

Mirror, Mirror

"Why do you look at the speck of sawdust in your brother's eye and pay no attention to the plank in your own eye?" (Matthew 7:3 NIV)

We have all heard that famous question in "Snow White and the Seven Dwarfs," where the evil queen asks a mirror "Who is the fairest one of all?" We also know the answer to that question—mirrors don't lie!

I had been using a local fitness center for several days when I finally took a good look at some of the others at the facility. I was aghast! They were a bunch of "old ladies!" Instantly I thought, "What am I doing here? I certainly don't belong! And I've even signed a contract!"

Fussing and fretting about this shocking discovery, I walked into the "cool-down" room to begin the prescribed stretching routine. Suddenly, a wall-sized mirror appeared. Had it always been there? Of course, it had! I stopped, stared intently at the mirror, only to discover an even more disturbing sight—I too, was one of those "old ladies!" Promptly finishing and leaving the facility, I mumbled under my breath, "but, I'm NOT as OLD as most of them." Quickly, I realized that although I look in the mirror every day, I really don't see the many changes happening to me.

Often, we are fast to see faults and imperfections in others yet fail to see the same or even more egregious deficiencies in ourselves. It's interesting that we often have solutions for their shortcomings, but neglect to recognize and even make excuses for our own. We berate self-righteous and critical attitudes in others, but justify the same in ourselves. After all, we're entitled to our opinion and we would rather not admit that we are down-right judgmental. Jesus used an exaggerated depiction of us to emphasize this point. To illustrate the blindness we often have to our own sins and faults, He spoke about how we can be critical of a minute "speck of sawdust" in someone else's eye, but fail to recognize the large "plank" in our own (v. 3). I was abruptly reminded that when we find ourselves criticizing, we should first take a careful look in the mirror. We might be surprised to see the very same or worse flaws and sins in our own lives. It may be a startling revelation, but at the same time, it is an opportunity to repent and work at changing our attitudes.

—Juanita Adamson

Money: Blessing or Curse?

"For the love of money is the root of all sorts of evil, and some
by longing for it have wandered away from the faith and pierced
themselves with many grieves." (1 Timothy 6:10 NASB)

Money is the root of all evil. Right? Wrong!!!

As the devil does in many cases, he causes a fallen world to believe misquotations and partial quotations. The Bible tells us—and more specifically—Paul writes to Timothy, his protégé, in First Timothy 6:10 the following:

> "For the love of money is the root of all sorts of evil, and
> some by longing for it have wandered away from the faith
> and pierced themselves with many grieves."

Money does not change who or what we are. It merely magnifies our basic beliefs. Our level of generosity, stewardship and prudence are not determined by how much or how little we have. More importantly, it does not determine how happy we are.

If we are suddenly flushed with a large amount of money, for example, by inheritance, winnings, as a young athlete, success in the market, an award from a court, a business which finally takes off or a gift from someone, it is God's way of showing us our level of faith in Him or showing, first hand, who we are to Him. It is not the amount of money that we make or have that is important. It is important that we recognize that it all belongs to God. It is only by His grace that we have it to enjoy and to use for His work here on earth.

If we recognize this, it will be a blessing—otherwise, it will be a curse.

—Jerry and Jane Hatfield

My Alabaster Jar

"While he was in Bethany, reclining at the table in the home of Simon the Leper, a woman came with an alabaster jar of very expensive perfume, made of pure nard. She broke the jar and poured the perfume on his head..." (Mark 14:3 NIV)

As I read this account in the Book of Mark about the alabaster jar containing a costly ointment that a woman lavished on Jesus as an act of worship, I began to think about those I value most. The balm in the jar represented a year's salary, perhaps her dowry. It was the most cherished item she owned and could very well have impacted her future. As I continued to read, a question quickly entered my mind— "Why is it so difficult to give up or surrender loved ones to Jesus?" I now realize that the question is impossible to answer even under good circumstances. And the response becomes even more complicated and incomprehensible when the situation sours.

When my mother was hospitalized before her death, we prayed for divine healing. She had been critically ill for several days. Because of her age and the difficulties encountered in quickly diagnosing the illnesses, we were told that she probably would not survive. I immediately began to bargain with God to let her live five more years. After all, another five years was a brief time in comparison to all of eternity!

Now, I look back and wonder—"what made me think I could negotiate with God? What made me believe I would be able to handle the grief of her loss any better in five years?" I don't have an answer. In my defense, all I can say is that I was desperate.

As the days went by, her condition worsened. Although we continued to pray, it became clearly apparent that God had chosen another path for her. My prayers, however, would be answered. She would receive healing, but just not here on earth.

After a distressing night, her team of doctors came to the room and sadly said, "We have done all we know to do, but nothing is working. Her organs are beginning to shut down. We can continue to treat her, but it will only prolong the agony she is experiencing. It's your decision."

I felt my heart shatter like a piece of fine crystal dashed to the floor. Shards were all that remained—they could never be put together again. My immediate thought was: "It isn't fair! Why my mom?"

The doctor needed confirmation of a decision she had made for herself fourteen years prior when a similar decision was made for Dad. Her Living Will expressed that she did not want heroic measures to keep her alive. But, could I confirm her decision? Could I trust God? Could I give Him my precious "alabaster jar?" Standing in the hallway, I knew what my mother would want. I had heard it so many times in recent months. She would get this "faraway" look in her eyes and say, "Mija,[7] I want to go home to be with Jesus and your dad. It's time—I'm tired."

Nonetheless, my heart struggled as I whispered, "God, why do I have to make the decision?" The decision had already been made by Mom—a confirmation was all that was needed as part of hospital policy. I looked at my siblings and they both whispered, "Let Mom go!"

Their words reverberated in my head. How could I do that? All I had to do was agree to have treatment stopped and Mom would go home to heaven, the goal of all Christians. Oh, it's easy enough to talk or sing about going to heaven to be with Jesus when not faced with the imminent prospect. But when the battle between life and death is waging, it's a grueling and painful challenge to give up our "alabaster jar" (our loved ones) to Jesus, who, in reality, loves them more than we do.

That decisive morning, I fully understood that God was in control of my mom's life. The document I was affirming was just a formality, having no impact on the will of God. Treatment stopped and she went home to be with Jesus less than two days later.

Has it been easy? No, I still miss my mom greatly—it has been more than six years. But I found a "not-so-secret" secret—we can rest

---

[7] Note: "Mija" is a Spanish term of endearment meaning "my daughter" and is short for "mi hija."

upon the truth of the gospel that Mom is finally really happy in the presence of Jesus and with loved ones, those having gone ahead of her. We too are promised a home in heaven, because of salvation through Jesus Christ. We can look forward to one day having a wonderful reunion with Jesus and our loved ones—our "alabaster jars."

—Juanita Adamson

My Laughing Place

*"A merry heart doeth good like a medicine; but a broken
spirit drieth the bones." (Proverbs 17:22 KJV)*

A Mayo Clinic Healthy Lifestyle article says that "When it comes to
relieving stress, more giggles and guffaws are just what the doctor
ordered"[8]

These noted physicians say that laughter can stimulate many organs,
activate and relieve your stress response, and soothe tension, among
many other beneficial results. It would appear that the author of this
article had already read the memo from the Lord, as indicated in
the Scripture shown above, that "a merry heart doeth good like a
medicine."

In the Bible, God has given remedies for all of the issues we will
ever encounter in life. We just need to take time to find them. One of
the greatest of such remedies has been the capacity for me to find my
own personal laughing place where I go for shelter in the midst of many
challenges in life—to restore health to "the bones."

In the 1946 Disney musical film, "Song of The South," one of the
characters, Br'er Rabbit, explains to Br'er Bear that "everyone's got a
laughing place... Trouble is most folks won't take the time to go look
for it."[9]

So where is your laughing place? That place where you can sing
yourself happy. Where you can sing the praises of God, even in "a
strange land" (see Psalm 137:4)—a place where you feel lost and don't
know which way to turn. Remember that wherever it is God will be
there, as Psalm 22:3 says that He "inhabits the praises of His people."
It's also the place where you can even laugh at your own mistakes,
knowing that your heavenly Father understands your frailties and will

---

[8] www.mayoclinic.org/healthy-living/stress-management
[9] www.songofthesouth.net/movie/lyrics.music; Music by Alice Wrubel, Lyrics by
Ray Gilbert ©Walt Disney Music Company 1946; See also disney.wikia.com/wiki/
Brer_Rabbit and Disney.wikia.com/wiki/Brer_Bear.

come to bring His perfect medicine—His joy and laughter—into your heart again.

I have learned that when I go to my laughing place in those sometimes-unsettling occasions, the situation may not change right away, but it can certainly change the way I view it while I'm waiting for God's complete healing—His sufficient grace.

—Phyllis Andrews

Obey Him in the Little Things

"He who is faithful in a very little thing, is
faithful also in much." (Luke 16:10 AMP)

Have you ever wanted to take on some really big project in the kingdom of God, but the Lord just wouldn't seem to let you? If so, there's probably a good reason why.

You can see what I'm talking about by reading what God did with the children of Israel after He brought them out of Egypt. He wanted to take them on into the Promised Land. But before He could do it, God had to know if they would obey Him. He had to know if they would listen to His voice. Because if they didn't, the enemies they were about to face would wipe them out.

So, you know what He did? He tested them in a small matter. Exodus 16:4 AMP, tells us about this simple test. "Then said the Lord unto Moses, Behold, I will rain bread from heaven for you; and the people shall go out and gather a certain rate every day, that I may prove them, whether they will walk in my law, or no (see also Exodus16:1-28)." God took an insignificant matter, the food they ate—and used it to see if they would listen to Him or not. He told them how much of it to gather, when to gather and when not to gather, and what to do with it after they brought it in. However, the Israelites went right out and violated those instructions. They showed God by their actions that His voice was not important to them. They were not willing to obey even His simplest commands. God works the same way today. Before he sends you on a major mission, He gives you the opportunity to prove you can be trusted with small instructions.

But many of us miss that opportunity. We pray, "What do you want me to do Lord? Where do you want me to go? I'll do anything You say." But then if the Lord says, "I want you to get up and pray one hour every morning," we fail to obey Him. We say, "Oh yeah, that would be good; I ought to do that." But somehow we never quite get around to it.

We should not make that mistake.

Start today obeying God in the little things. Let Him know that He can trust you out there in a place of much authority. Let Him know you will be faithful to His Words and to the voice of His Spirit.

He may just start sending bigger assignments your way.

—Tancy Elliott

Silver Legs

"Therefore, as God's chosen people, holy and dearly loved,
clothe yourselves with compassion, kindness, humility,
gentleness and patience." (Colossians 3:12 NIV)

Thirteen children under six, twenty-six little hands and thirteen glue sticks—a recipe for disaster! As frustration grew, I attempted to remain calm. I silently prayed, "Jesus, help me!" But, it seemed that help was not on its way. Quite the contrary, failure was just a silver leg away.

I had planned a wonderful craft to reinforce the Bible lesson of the day—"card stock ants," to illustrate the wisdom of one of God's tiniest creatures. The evening before, I carefully cut out fifteen ant bodies from green card stock and thirty legs and thirty antennae from silver chenille sticks. After making a sample, I decided that yes, it was the perfect illustration, a cute reminder of the lesson. I was so excited for my class of 3 to 5 year olds to see my "little ant." I, however, neglected to remember the curious nature and uncoordinated movements of young children. No sooner had "the ant" been placed on the table, than a rambunctious four-year old grabbed it and quickly smashed it! When "the ant" was rescued, it could no longer stand on its legs.

I looked at it in dismay as I handed out supplies. After a short time and many annoyed cries for help, I abandoned the project—my patience ran out. The children in their eagerness would not let the glue dry so the silver legs and antennae continued to fall off. The "ants" were never able to stand up like I had expected; in fact, the legs fell off no matter what we did. The project was a total failure yet the kids wanted to take them home.

For weeks, silver legs or antennae were found on the church grounds as evidence of my absurd attempt at making ants. Yet in all the confusion and defeat God faithfully reminded me of the times when I have given my problems to Him and then taken them back. In my own eagerness and impatience, I've decided to help Him fix my difficulties. And, just like the children refusing to wait for the glue to set up on the chenille sticks, I often struggle allowing God to formulate and cement solutions for my circumstances.

Our loving and enduring Father reminded me that He has the right solutions—the only answers for us. However, one question seems to remain, "Will we ever have enough patience or trust to wait on Him for our answers?"

—Juanita Adamson

The Burning Bush

"And the angel of the Lord appeared unto him in a flame of fire out
of the midst of a bush; and he looked, and, behold, the bush burned
with fire, and the bush was not consumed." (Exodus 3:2 KJV)

I have often wondered why God chose to appear to Moses from
within a burning bush. A recent sermon by our pastor clarified
this. Investigation has revealed that these bushes were apparently
commonplace in the desert. Due to the blistering desert heat, it was
not uncommon for a bush to catch fire and quickly become a pile of
smoldering ashes. Therefore, Moses, after forty years of shepherding
sheep in the desert would not have been surprised to see a burning
bush. But this bush was different! The fire did not consume it—the
ordinary became extraordinary.

Fascinated by this spectacle, Moses stepped closer to inspect this
oddity further. God called out to Moses from within the bush and
warned him to come no further and to remove his sandals, as the place
upon which he stood was holy ground.

God also takes the mundane and ordinary in our life and calls to
us. The ordinary becomes divine.

Do we hear Him or are we too busy to hear? Do we hear Him, but
make excuses like Moses did concerning his ability to serve the Lord?
Do we hear Him, but try to do it in our own strength, retreating into
our own preconceived notions of behavior? Do not miss your burning
bush. If you see it, do not make excuses. If you take action, do not do
it in your own strength, but walk in God's strength and will. Then you,
the ordinary, will become extraordinary in Him. The burning bush of
God will dwell within you! Others will see the light of God's burning
bush shining forth from you. You will be a light to the world as you
walk with Jesus, onward and into the eternity of the Promised Land.

—Catherine Ricks Urbalejo

The Grand Canyon

"In the beginning God created the heavens
and the earth." (Genesis 1:1 NIV)

If you ever want to experience an example of God's power, beauty, and splendor, visit the Grand Canyon here in Arizona!

There is no place on Earth with more magnificence. It changes every minute of the day. The sun rises and brings the soft pastel colors that float through the canyon. The pinks, mauves, oranges, and blues softly spread the breathtaking colors from one end to the other. As the sun rises higher, the peaks turn to shades of beige and brown with green trees spotted here and there. The puffy white clouds drift in and out. They gather and darken until the white flash of lightening cuts them open and the rain falls into the river beneath where you stand. The thunder roars as the flashes of light dance through the sky. As it slows, a rainbow appears down in the canyon—lending more color to an unbelievable watercolor. The sun sets and the clouds that linger turn to fiery orange and pink. The further the sun drops the richer the color. The sky is on fire.

When night draws near, the sky is splattered with the moon and stars that God flung to the heavens. The canyon is truly a wonder from God—and His gift to us is to behold it.

—Sue Walker

Up to Seven Times?

"Then Peter came to Him and said, 'Lord, how often shall my brother sin against me, and I forgive him? Up to seven times?' Jesus said to him, 'I do not say to you up to seven times, but up to seventy times seven.'" (Matthew18: 21–22 NKJV)

"I felt so betrayed!" "I thought she was my friend, or they were my trusted co-workers! How could she (or he) have done this to me or said that about me? But, aha, I could do (or say) such and such to get even!"

Have thoughts of retaliation, or revenge crossed your mind after some terrible incident occurred, where you were hurt or betrayed? If I was to answer that question honestly, I would have to say "yes." I have experienced situations causing similar thoughts to beleaguer my mind—my whole being. Unfortunately, instead of quickly forgiving, as the Bible tells me, I have focused on the person or circumstances and, perhaps, even formulated a plan of vengeance. Quickly, my whole life became consumed by the minute details of the situation. My attention seemed to dwell on the incident almost without respite. But, you know, I don't think I'm alone.

Evidently Peter, the disciple, had a similar problem because he asked Jesus, "Lord, how often shall my brother sin against me, and I forgive him? Up to seven times?" Jesus quickly answered him, not only seven times but up to "seventy times seven." In other words, as many times as might become necessary. It's interesting to note that Jesus didn't ask Peter the severity or subject of the offense. So, it's clear that those details really don't matter. Large, small or repeated violations, we have no other choice than to forgive—and the sooner the better. Holding grudges and retribution are clearly NOT optional. And yes, forgiveness at times is difficult, but not impossible when God helps us reconcile our hurts.

So our choice, the next time someone offends or hurts us, is to quickly forgive them like the Bible undeniably tells us.

—Juanita Adamson

What Are You Growing Through?

"Consider it pure joy, my brothers and sisters, whenever
you face trials of many kinds, because you know that
the testing of your faith produces perseverance. Let
perseverance finish its work so that you may be mature and
complete, not lacking anything." (James 1:2–4 NIV)

What are you growing through? What is the situation that you have been going through that God is trying to get you to grow through? You see, God doesn't want us to be going through anything, but to be growing through everything. When we begin to see the trial before us as an opportunity rather than an obstacle, we can have peace through the storm and come to a realization of God's enduring grace. God is continually trying to mold your character through circumstances and has your best interest in mind. He won't let you come undone. He called you into this situation and will lead you out of it through growth in your character. Stop resisting the trial and embrace it for what God is trying to teach you. When it seems like God is not doing something for you, He is most likely doing something in you.

God loves you and has a great plan for your future. That is why He has to prepare you through this trial. When it seems like the trial will never end, you will be delivered. Then, you will be able to sit down and write, "What I have learned through this trial." And, it will be some of the greatest wisdom of your life.

Your best years are ahead of you, so embrace what you are growing through and allow your character to be enriched enough to handle His blessings that chase the ones who allow His work to be completed in them.

—Rev. James D. Moore

What Do You See?

"Then he turned to his disciples privately and said, 'Blessed are the eyes that see what you see.'" (Luke 10:23 NIV)

Have you ever wondered how the elderly might feel as they age and lose independence? Listen with an open heart. Having worked in skilled nursing facilities where God directed me for thirty years, this phrase was heard many times as the patients grew older and frailer from illness - "I shouldn't have to live this long." I put it into a poem and have never shared it until now:

"I Shouldn't Have To Live This Long"

They look with faded eyes and wrinkles
etched deep into their faces –
- *"I shouldn't have to live this long"*
Betrayed by their bodies
No longer able to go the distance
Families who are unable or afraid to
acknowledge the culmination
of full circle
- *"I shouldn't have to live this long"*
Dependent on others now
Where before fierce independence once flourished
"Could you help me please? I've waited so long."
Bingo, worship at church services, oldies
but goodies, park and walk
All to keep the highest level of function
- *"But I shouldn't have to live this long"*
The days go by with little change other than
skin grows more fragile, appetite less
Things that seemed important no longer are
The highlights of the day are breakfast, lunch, and dinner

- *"I shouldn't have to live this long"*
Does God Listen?
Maybe tomorrow I can go
Please understand --*"I shouldn't have to live this long."*

Remember them and hold them close to your heart. Be their spokesperson, their guardian, and the light in their day. Remind them that God has a plan.

—Sue Walker

Whose Hands Are These?

"Whatsoever your hand finds to do, do it with
all your might." (Ecclesiastes 9:10 ESV)

It is after midnight and I stand barefoot on the cold tiles; the bathroom light casts its glow on my outstretched arms.

Whose hands are these, I wonder? Mine? Where was I when they grew to look like this?

I remember laughingly saying that the ends of my index fingers point to the left and the right instead of straight ahead. I've been careful to speak directions to avoid sending some poor soul around the corner following the curve of my wayward pointers.

I often explain, with tongue in cheek, that my fingers curve on the ends to precisely apply makeup to the inside corners of my eyes.

I also remember the knots on the ends of my "pointing fingers." Goodness, I've had those for a long time, but suddenly I find they have grown and spread to all my fingers.

This jolt came during a recent doctor's exam as he sagely mentioned the arthritis in my fingers. "Oh, no, you're wrong," I sputtered. "I don't have arthritis. They don't even hurt!" Actually, when you reach my age most everything hurts—so it's easy to miss the exact location.

When did my fingers begin to gnarl? This is all such a surprise to me. As I examine them here in the quiet, dim light, I begin to notice the knots, the wrinkles, and the age spots that have crept in every crease. An epiphany! They have been at the end of my arms all along! Sure, I've noticed a few things changing here and there, but I've never taken the time to study them because these hands are seldom still.

"An epiphany," I said. Have you noticed our tendency to exaggerate words? It's like there is no height left to describe a real wonder. We've used them all up describing the awesome hotdog we had at the ball park. Following these thoughts, I looked up the word "epiphany." In this case, I believe I got it right. The Encarta Dictionary: English

(North America) describes it as a sudden intuitive leap of understanding especially through an ordinary, but striking occurrence.

My epiphany—better known to Christians as a message being taught by the Holy Spirit—began with the following: "Whatever you do, work heartedly, as for the Lord and not for men knowing that from the Lord you will receive the inheritance as your reward you are serving the Lord Christ (Colossians 3:23–24 ESV)."

My hands are God's hands! They are always busy, moving here and there; assisting, calming, serving, holding, stroking, patting, mending, reviving, relieving, supporting—and clasping in prayer.

Yes, I decide, when I gaze at my hands, it's a good thing. I see my mother's hands and my Granny's hands, too. As I consider them, I'm really not distressed anymore by the changes I see. I'm honored to be like them—both physically and spiritually.

There is a special blessing—a bond to being like them or connected to them—A circle of women selected by God.

—Jane Hatfield

~ Section 4 ~
ABOUNDING GRACE

"He waters the mountains from His upper rooms;
the earth is satisfied and abounds with the fruit of His works."

(Psalm 104:13 AMP)

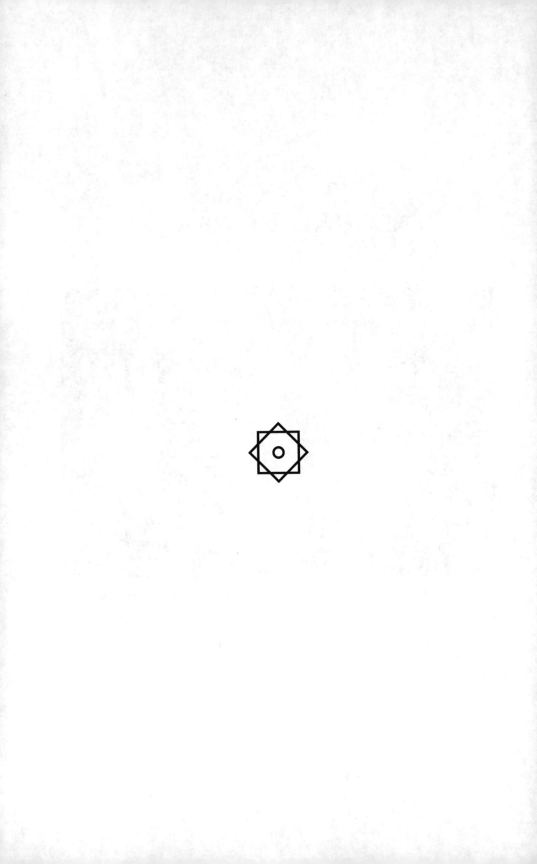

A Moment In Time

"See what great love the Father has lavished on us, that we should be called children of God! And that is what we are." (1 John 3:1 NIV)

Cherished moments in God's presence occur when we least expect them. It was a beautiful, warm autumn day in southeast Arizona. As night-time temperatures dropped, the leaves were turning brilliant shades of red, yellow, rust, and brown. It was a glorious day—a day perfect for hiking and a picnic with friends.

After unloading our food items at one of the Carr Canyon picnic areas, some of our group decided to hike to the ruins of the old ranch. We crossed a stream (it had water) and a lovely meadow of tall grass. The morning breezes rhythmically moved the blades as if they were performing a lovely waltz. I wondered if anyone noticed the dance recital God provided or were they so intent on reaching our destination to see anything but the trail ahead. Purposely, I lagged behind.

Soon, we reached the ruins. The stone walls—covered with decades of ivy—held secrets of those living there many years ago. Choosing to remain alone to meditate on God's goodness, I sat on the old ranch house staircase. Feeling the sun's warmth delicately caressing my face, I closed my eyes. I felt enveloped in a blanket of peace and security. Opening my eyes, I slowly took a refreshing drink of cool water, enjoying its wetness as it flowed through my parched lips. I looked at God's wonderful creation—tall craggy mountains with cliffs and outcroppings, a myriad of colored vegetation, rugged ancient trees with vines like satin ribbons circling their thick trunks and limbs, the cloudless cerulean sky, tall swaying grass, insects darting amidst the trees, and an occasional bird calling its mates.

Momentarily, everything seemed brighter, sharper and more exquisite than I had noticed before. My senses, my spirit, were more sensitive, more aware. With a new perspective, I felt overwhelmed looking at God's majestic creation, trying to capture it all in my mind. Again closing my eyes, I felt God's arms of love encircle me as I sat quietly. I heard a whisper—"everything is alright." "Alright," the word reverberated in my spirit.

Then, as if suspended in time, the moment was broken; someone called my name. It was time to go. But, for an instant, I felt "the great love the Father lavished" on me—just me, His child—my private moment with my heavenly Father! Those moments alone with God make all the difference in our day and in our lives. Interrupt your busyness and take time to savor His goodness and the love He lavishes on us—"children of God."

—Juanita Adamson

Answered Prayer

"And the prayer of faith will save the sick and the
Lord will raise him up..." (James 5:15 NKJV)

I stand here—"To God be the Glory"—as an example of how powerful the love and prayers of Christian sisters and brothers can be when we join together as one spirit.

I went from having "no hope" because the doctors told me I did not have a chance. They weren't sure that they could keep me alive. It was touch-and-go, a long hospital stay, and many complications that I knew were spiritual attacks. With my spirit in gear, I prayed diligently every waking moment, and I felt the hand of the Lord. My church family also prayed for me.

My primary care doctor questioned the diagnosis given by the hospital physicians. After further examination and tests, they changed the diagnosis and cancelled the liver transplant. In my heart, the old diagnosis was correct, but the new diagnosis was "I AM HEALED." I believe that this happened when I surrendered my cares and burdens to Jehovah Rapha, the Lord who heals.

So many times we ask God, "Why me?" instead of, "Look at God – WOW!" "Thank you God for choosing me to sit down and spend time with You. You put a halt to my busy life so I could bask in your Word and get to know You better. My faith is growing and maturing through suffering and endurance, knowing the prize at the end. Thank you for life!"

—Cathi Rumbaugh

But God

"Then I bathed you with water, washed off your blood from
you and anointed you with oil." (Ezekiel 16:9 NASB)

My walk of faith in so many ways parallels that of Israel and her journey
with God. In Isaiah 5, Israel is compared to a vine that brought forth
wild grapes. In Hosea 10, she is likened to an empty vine. In Chapter
15 of Ezekiel, the Lord sees her as a worthless vine. My life before I
came to the Lord Jesus was a rebellious and wild experience based
upon my desires, plans, and concerns; entirely self-centered with never
a thought for God.

After entering into my thirties—married and a mother of two
children—I found myself unsatisfied with my life and questioning
the future of my career goals and the man I had chosen as my life
partner. I was frustrated, tired and empty, and asking "Is that
all there is?" I am quite sure that the Lord had assessed all my
efforts and works up to that time as worthless and unfruitful for
His Kingdom. "BUT GOD"—that is my favorite expression from
Scripture. When all seems dark, bleak and hopeless, and we are
at the end of ourselves, that is exactly when God can bring His
light, His hope, and His purpose into our hearts and change us
for His glory.

FOUND: "I found you. I took care of you. And then I made you
beautiful;" God says to Israel in the 16th chapter of Ezekiel. What God
prefigured and accomplished for Israel—He has mercifully performed
over my life. I was born in sin, rebellious against God, and left to die.
But God came to me as I lay near spiritual death, and said "Live!" Now,
He has washed me with the water of His Word (Ephesians 5:26) and
with His shed blood (Hebrews 13:12). He has anointed me with the oil
of the Holy Spirit (Psalm 23:5). I am clothed with the linen of Christ's
righteousness (Isaiah 61:10), the silk of His own beauty (Psalm 149:4),
and God has given me Life in Christ.

ME: Fifteen years ago, I was baptized at the age of forty-eight and was gifted to go on a mission trip to Guatemala that year. The following year God enabled me to visit Israel with my son who was baptized there in the River Jordan. Our daughter is on a journey once more with Jesus and the Lord has shown favor to my husband and to our marriage.

As we follow the Lord in obedience, His Holy Spirit abides with us,
Building our spirit so that our desire to know Him increases,
He delights and deepens our walk of faith—

Let's follow and go deep!

—Cathy Avila

Christmas Angel

"Do not forget to entertain strangers for by so doing some people have entertained angels without knowing it." (Hebrews 13:2 NIV)

It was December 2013. My friend and I went to the Salvation Army Thrift Store to look around, as we did several times a week. As we walked in, all I could think about was wishing I had the means to buy my granddaughter a Christmas present. However, I had no money for gifts. I then thought about the beautiful Christmas sweaters I used to wear when I sang for the Lord during the holidays in church and other places. They were all destroyed in storage during the monsoon season.

I was talking to my friend about wanting to get my granddaughter something and a Christmas sweater for myself, but I only had five dollars. We were in the clothing department with only two other women looking through the racks. The people were scarce that day, I remember thinking, Next thing I knew, someone tapped me on the shoulder and said, "Excuse me?" I turned around and this lady who had not been in the store or the clothing department had a ten dollar bill in her hand. She said, "Take this and get your granddaughter something for Christmas and a Christmas sweater for yourself." I said, "Oh no, that's okay," as I wondered where she came from. She placed the ten dollars in my hand. I turned my head around to my friend, saying "I met this lady who just gave me this money," but as I turned back around, the lady had disappeared. My friend questioned, "Where is she?" I answered, "I don't know, she's gone. Maybe she was an angel—you know how the Bible talks about meeting angels unaware (see Hebrews 13:2)!"

After this blessing, we started searching for a nice blouse or sweater for my granddaughter. As we were looking in separate aisles, I heard my friend say, "Here's a Christmas sweater!" Sure enough the sweater was festive, beautiful and yes, my size. By the time we finished I had found not one, but two blouses and one sweater for my granddaughter—all in her favorite color. I was overjoyed and thanked

God for sending *one of His angels* to fulfill my Christmas wishes. I will never forget God's miracles, especially at Christmas. I was even asked to sing at the Salvation Army party and of course I wore my new Christmas sweater.

Have you ever met a ministering angel? I believe I have.

—Lynne Brown

Crazy Old People

"Those who are planted in the house of the LORD shall flourish
in the courts of our God. They shall still bear fruit in old age;
They shall be fresh and flourishing." (Psalm 92:13–14 NKJV)

The headline in an Italian newspaper read: "Man, 87, escapes a care home 'full of old people' and flees down a motorway in his electric wheelchair." He reportedly said that at the care center everyday was the same and lacked adventure.

Similarly, Caleb, one of my favorite Bible characters, is the one who at 80+ years old refused the offer of a less-challenging part of the Promised Land in preference for a more risky mountainous region for his inheritance. It was also said of Caleb that his name means "dog," which could have meant that at one point in his life he was "as mean as a junkyard dog" [I'm still laughing].

Many of us have also heard the stories of super-elderly people, including a former President of the United States, who have even engaged in dangerous sports, such as skydiving [now that's really crazy].

Contemporary "self-help" gurus like Les Brown and Christiane Northrop further indicate that we are never too old to set another goal or dream a new dream. Even Moses and his brother Aaron were both octogenarians when God sent them to speak to Pharaoh and demand that he let the Israelites leave Egypt (see Exodus 7:1–7).

So maybe you can't walk as far or as fast as you used to. Then get the best, top-of-the-line wheelchair you can afford and go fishing with the group. In fact, one of the residents of the local nursing care center can often be found on his way to the Mall, the local Starbucks, or just to see the sights in his motorized chair [one good electric charge and he's on his way].

Yes, it is definitely a fact that as we age our physical strength begins to fade and our mental acuity may deteriorate somewhat (see Ecclesiastes 12:1-7), but let's try not to lose our zest for life and a willingness to seek new adventures. The Bible promises that we can still be "fresh and flourishing" in old age (Psalm 92:14).

I think I would prefer to believe the Bible, rather than grumbling away my final years in complacency. What do you think?

—Phyllis Andrews

Fathers

"Behold, what manner of love the Father hath bestowed upon us, that we should be called the sons of God: therefore the world knoweth us not, because it knew him not." (1 John 3:1 KJV)

"Catherine, the best gift I can give to you is an education," said my father to my young self in the tumultuous sixties. "No matter what happens in this life you will be able to take care of yourself." True to his word he paid for my education, even continuing throughout graduate school when I was already in my early thirties. My father was always there for me no matter what. Today, long after his passing, I have been blessed with a great career and continued part-time work through retirement— even in the current economic environment. For this sound wisdom and solid foundation I will be forever grateful to my earthly father.

Many years have passed. I am much older now. I have become more vibrantly aware in the deepest part of my being that I have another Father—a spiritual Father. Just as I had a personal relationship with my earthly father so also I have a personal relationship with my heavenly Father. This heavenly Father I am privileged to call "Abba" or Daddy. I talk to Him often as I go about my daily life! This Father has revealed through His Word, His Holy Spirit and other Christians that I will have internal peace and joy in this life no matter my circumstances. As long as we hold fast to Him, He has promised that He will work out our circumstances for our ultimate good. And there is more. I have the blessed hope of eternal life with my spiritual Father after death! I am not afraid of death's sting—"Are you afraid of death?"

If death frightens you, repent of your sins, trust in the Lord Jesus Christ as your Lord and Savior, as the only way to the triune God (Father, Son, and Holy Spirit) and begin your new and eternal life today!

—Catherine Ricks Urbalejo

Footprints

"And in all things showing yourself to be a pattern
of good works; in doctrine showing integrity,
reverence, incorruptibility." (Titus 2:7 NKJV)

Wherever we go and whatever we do, we leave footprints of our presence. For example, when a large building is demolished the footprint of its foundation is left as an historical testimony of where it once stood. My cat's footprints in the dust on my table are also a tell-tale sign of where she has been when we were away from the house. In Budapest, Poland, sixty pairs of shoes have been cast in iron by artists and permanently affixed on the edge of the Danube River to commemorate the lives and steps of Holocaust victims. The shoes are crafted in different sizes and styles to represent the children, women, businessmen, sportsmen, etc., who were forced to strip naked on the banks of the Danube—where a firing squad shot them at close range. This was to ensure that they would simply fall into the river and be washed away.

After reading that story, I also saw the line of shoes on the shore as "footprints" of the ultimate price their owners paid for their moral and religious convictions between 1944 and 1945.

In everyday life, Christians are called to show themselves as patterns of good works, but sadly some of our family members have imprints of our shoes on their faces, on their backs, and noticeably on their hearts and minds.

Our footprints may have resulted in depressed wives and broken children. They are wives who would rather "go it alone" with their children than to suffer daily mental and often physical abuse. They are children who look like "deer in the headlights" when their names are routinely shouted or used profanely every day of their lives.

We often create the mess that our schoolteachers have to deal with on a daily basis. We step on our families at home and they reflect their pain on someone else at school or in the community. In Colossians 3:19, 21 NKJV, the Christian family is admonished as follows: "Husbands, love your wives, and be not bitter against them...Fathers provoke not your children to anger, lest they be discouraged." The home is to be a place of comfort and companionship—Not boot camp.

Accordingly, our goal should be to leave large, clear and loving footprints that are a pattern of good works for those who come behind us to walk in.

—Phyllis Andrews

Forgiveness

"If ye forgive men their trespasses, your heavenly Father will also forgive you: But if ye forgive not men their trespasses neither will your heavenly Father forgive your trespasses." (Matthew 6:14–15 KJV)

For – for all the people, who have done wrong to me;

Give – give them the same grace that God has given me;

Ness – provide what is necessary to get to heaven.

These three syllables when put together (Forgiveness) say a whole lot—Life or Death.

God created us in His image. He sent His only begotten Son to die for our sins. When we forgive our brethren, we glorify God. Forgiveness is one thing we can control even though our hearts may feel out of control.

Oh, how much we miss out on when we hold grudges. Not only does it make our hearts hard and stony, but it affects our physical health. We can put on makeup and wear the trendiest clothes, but inside we are crying and shedding tears like that faucet where we just washed our hands. But the peace, joy, and love of Jesus can be ours, if we choose to forgive.

Remember, we have all sinned against others, as well, and we must forgive and even pray for those who have done us wrong (see Matthew 5:44).

Jesus, a great example, walked this earth to teach us about love without regrets. Forgiveness is our choice.

—Cathi Rumbaugh

Forgiveness

"…[Love] keeps no record of wrongs." (1 Corinthians 13:5 NIV)

God's greatest gift of love to us is his Son, Jesus Christ. "For God so loved the world that he gave his one and only Son, that whoever believes in him shall not perish but have eternal life" (John 3:16). Can you imagine giving the life of your only son that others may live *(the ultimate sacrifice)*? God loves us even though we have sinned, and He tells us in the Bible to even love our neighbor as we love ourselves.

How much love do we have?

To love is to forgive all fault, then forget. But how do we do that when some wrongs are so horrendous that we may forgive, but it is very difficult to forget? We have to not allow the wrong to fester in our heart, which will ultimately encourage hate.

Love is a Jesus Christ-virtue. Accordingly, if you find it difficult to forgive and forget, offer it up in prayer and remember what Christ did for us. He offers forgiveness to all of us, and God has even forgotten our list of sins.

—Sue Walker

God's Magnificent Creations

"Be still and know that I am God." (Psalm 46:10 NIV)

I love watching birds fly—each flapping their wings at different momentums in order to travel wherever they need to go. As I observed them, I marveled how God created each kind in their own uniqueness. They have a built-in faith, never having to stop and think where they are going. They rely on their God-given instinct that shows them where to go.

God also made each and every one of us unique. He is always ready anytime, as I put my faith into action, to help me with whatever lies ahead. His presence is so sweet, so gentle, yet strong—encompassing me as I seek His guidance. I never want to let this feeling go.

I have found that the more I walk in the lordship of Christ, the more His presence lingers around me. I but close my eyes and feel the Holy Spirit within and around me. There is no such feeling like it anywhere—His presence so magnificent in all His glory.

—Lynne Brown

Hummingbirds

"But ask the animals, and they will teach you, or the birds
in the sky, and they will tell you;" (Job 12:7 NIV)

Have you ever had one of God's creations with which you seem to identify such as a bird, flower, trees, or butterfly?

My mother loved hummingbirds. We see them frequently in Southeast Arizona. Did you ever wonder if they could ever send you a message?

My mother's husband passed away less than two months after she passed. At his funeral, during the service conducted by the Chaplin, a little hummingbird flew right up to his chest that was full of brightly colored military ribbons. The Chaplin tried to make it go away, but it was very persistent. My brother, sister, and I all felt it was in some way a message from our mother.

Later we believe she also sent another message regarding my brother. He had moved to Arkansas and did not keep in touch with me. I later learned he had a large aortic aneurysm and was having surgery to correct it. I was very concerned. Then, one day when I was on my patio where I have a wind chime in which I had placed some of my mother's ashes, a little hummingbird came and fluttered around it for several minutes. It made me feel so calm. I just felt for certain that my brother would be fine. Sure enough he was.

The third "hummingbird message" came when I was dating the man I would marry. When you first realize you are in love, you want to share that feeling with your mother, but of course my mother was gone. However, one day when "my cowboy" and I were in Bisbee, Arizona, window shopping, we stopped to look at art work in a store window. Amazingly, right between us flew a little hummingbird. It fluttered there seemingly to look at the colorful art work along with us. Then, as quickly as it came, it was gone. I believe it was my mother's way of saying that the cowboy was okay!

My mother was my best friend and I miss her every day, but I believe that God gave me this very special gift in return. I know that He continually watches over me—and I believe that in some special way Mother does too.

—Sue Walker

Humongous

"In the same way, even though we are many people,
we are one body in the Messiah and individual parts
connected to each other." (Romans 12:5 ISV)

There is something magical about viewing a grove of quaking aspen trees clustered together in undulating patterns across mountain slopes. Each of the individual trees is said to be genetically identical, derived from one single original tree and connected by a single root system. A grove of aspen trees in Utah is believed to be the world's largest living plant. Although its genetic uniformity is questioned, a humongous fungus discovered in 1998 may be the world's largest known living organism covering 2,200 acres in Oregon.

Just off the coast of Queensland, Australia, is one of the wonders of the world—the Great Barrier Reef. Research indicates that this is believed to be the world's largest super organism. The reef structure itself is composed of billions of tiny life forms known as coral polyps, and is the home to a variety of plant and animal life living in harmony with the reef. However, these worldly structures created by God's own hand pale in comparison to the magnificence of the gigantic spiritual being of Christ's body – The Church. It is estimated that there are 2.18 billion Christians on this planet representing nearly one third of the total human population. I do not know how many are actually true believers, but those who are and those from preceding generations comprise an enormous spiritual organism of which Christ is the head. We are all connected as brothers and sisters in Christ, each with different roles within the one spiritual body encompassing the earth.

The root system of the quaking aspen trees reminds me of how all of us are "rooted" in Christ; the tree's genetic uniformity being a picture of how we are all uniform in Christ. The humongous fungus, reminds me of how we are individual human beings each beautifully genetically unique, yet connected together in Christ. The coral reef that provides support to other animals and plants reminds me how the spiritual house of the believing church supports, sustains, and reaches out into its communities. How comforting it is to know that I am not alone. I am connected to all the members of Christ's church, but most of all I am connected and one with Him.

Are you a member of Christ's Spiritual Body?

—Catherine Ricks Urbalejo

Impossible Task

"From the end of the earth will I cry unto thee,
when my heart is overwhelmed: lead me to the rock
that is higher than I." (Psalm 61:2 NIV)

About six years ago when the Women of Grace Writers began talking about writing a book of devotions, I thought to myself, "that is an impossible task! The other women may be gifted enough to write devotions, but me, what do I know? God doesn't give me any great insight."

My negative thoughts continued until one day the Holy Spirit reminded me that He would help and direct us if the book was His plan for us. After all, He is the God of the impossible! Although I continued to struggle with my fears and inadequacies, I kept praying, "If this is what you want us to do, Lord, help us, especially me. I'm willing but I need your help." And, help, He did!

Our first book of devotions, "Spirit Aflame," was published and was blessed to be sold and distributed worldwide. However, the struggles to write for the book were ever-present. Often, everything I wrote was deleted. The "delete key" became my constant companion. Other times, the words seemed to flow effortlessly. I felt the Holy Spirit's presence giving inspiration. He would prompt me to a scripture to study and meditate on or personal experience and the words would begin to course smoothly through my fingers unto the keyboard. I felt, without a doubt, that Jesus was involved. He had to be because I certainly couldn't take on this task alone.

It was a journey, difficult at times, yet rewarding because of what I was discovering about my relationship with Jesus. There was prayer, self-examination, and careful reflection of thoughts, behavior and circumstances in addition to the study of the Word. The Holy Spirit's spotlight on certain areas of my life resulted in a deeper, closer walk with Jesus, "the rock that is higher than I (v. 2)."

My trust and obedience to the God of the impossible increased. I began to realize that writing devotions was merely an act of submission— we were writing down God-given thoughts and our experiences in prayerful hope that they might help someone whose heart, like ours, is, at times, overwhelmed. There was no magic or extraordinary gifting to writing the devotions, just perseverance and obedience, on the part of several women, to the voice of Jesus.

Keep in mind that whenever our hearts are overwhelmed with those impossible, unsolvable situations or tasks, we can go to our rock, Jesus, for comfort and help.

—Juanita Adamson

Lifting As We Climb

"...Prepare in the wilderness the way of the Lord [clear away
the obstacles]; make straight and smooth in the desert a
highway for our God! Every valley shall be lifted and filled
up, and every mountain and hill shall be made low, and
the crooked and uneven shall be made straight and level,
and the rough places a plain. And the glory (majesty and
splendor) of the Lord shall be revealed, and all flesh shall
see it together, for the mouth of the Lord has spoken it."
(Isaiah 40:3–5 AMP)

John the Baptist, of whom this Scripture refers, was called to "prepare the way" for the coming Messiah, Jesus Christ. We too, who are called to believe in Jesus as our Savior and Lord have the same or similar awesome task of preparing the hearts of people in our generation for the second coming of our Lord. "Every valley must be filled"— the poor and lowly must be raised up; the "mountains" of pride and self-righteousness must be humbled; "the crooked" and dishonest must be convinced of the error of their ways, and the hearts of the rough and rude must become pliable and courteous. Only when the moral nature of man becomes alive and renewed by the Spirit of God will we be able to see the true glory of God—it will surely be revealed, because God Himself has spoken it.

So the special work of John the Baptist, which we emulate, was to prepare the way of our Lord by a spiritual change in the heart, mind and character of those to whom he ministered. So do we need the ability to recite the scriptures from Genesis to Revelation and carry an extra-large-print-black-King James-version of the Bible under our arm to "prepare the way" of the Lord for others? Are we expected to walk about in animal skins and eat locust and wild honey while preaching repentance as did John the Baptist? Of course not! In John 12:32, we learn that if we lift up Christ to the world by simply sharing how our lives have been changed through His love, mercy, and grace – then He "will draw all men" unto Himself. One of my favorite hymns also says it plainly: "Lift Him up by living as a Christian ought; Let the world in you the Savior see; Then men will gladly follow Him who once taught, I'll draw all men unto Me." [10]

—Phyllis Andrews

---

[10] Lift Him Up;" Oatman, Jr., Johnson, 1903, Public Domain; library.timelesstruths. org/music/Lift_Him_Up/

Mother's Lavender Mum

"You are the God who performs miracles; you display
your power among the peoples." (Psalm 77:17 NIV)

On April 25, 1964, my mother died at the young age of forty-seven. She went into the hospital to have a spot removed from her right lung. Both of her lungs were cancerous; she died the third day after her surgery. God spared her the agony of a painful life.

There were so many flowers at her funeral. She was a godly woman and loved by everyone she met. All the flowers stacked on top of her grave were enormous. A friend of our extended family took a pot of lavender mums home with her. Lavender was mother's favorite color.

The mum was placed in the neighbor's flower garden. She was often awarded "Yard of Month." Mother was always in awe of her garden. The mum stayed alive, but never re-bloomed despite the tender-loving care the neighbor gave it. The following year on the morning of May 23, 1965, a new bloom appeared; the day I graduated from high school. "What a coincidence," people exclaimed, as news of the new bloom spread over the small town.

Like before, the mum didn't bloom again. That is, not until June 26, 1966, my wedding day. "That's unbelievable," people exclaimed again! However, as our neighbor came through the reception line she whispered in my ear that the mum had indeed bloomed again. I couldn't help but wonder if this was a miracle. Was this Mother's way of letting me know she shared in my joy on both important days of my life? Yes, to me this was a miracle. As before, the mum stayed alive and healthy, yet never bloomed again.

In 1968, my husband and I were in Japan awaiting the birth of our baby. On July 29, 1968, the long-awaited day arrived and, much to our amazement, we were blessed with identical twin girls! The doctor never heard two heartbeats until I went into labor. Amazingly, when our neighbor got up that morning she found *two* blooms on the mum plant. She immediately called my father, and excitedly asked,

"Did Lynne have her baby today?" He said, "You won't believe this, but she just gave birth to twin girls!" The neighbor told Dad about the two blooms on the mum plant, exclaiming "This could not be a coincidence, Millard!" He had been skeptical before, but then he had to admit that it was impossible to ignore. The whole town was in amazement and rejoiced. I believe in my heart that this was Mother's way of letting me know she shared in the special times of my life; that she shared in our abundant joy!

The mum plant lived for years. However, to my knowledge, it never bloomed again.

—Lynne Brown

"My Mommy is Lost"

"And let our own [people really] learn to apply themselves to good deeds...so that they may be able to meet necessary demands whenever the occasion may require..." (Titus 3:14 AMP)

During the Christmas shopping days last year, I had an occasion to be a first responder. For those of you who may not fully understand what that means, a first responder is someone designated or trained to respond to an emergency.

The emergency, in my case, was in the form of one of the most beautiful, angelic-looking little boys I had ever seen. He was just rambling down an aisle in Walmart, mumbling to himself. Other shoppers also saw him, but I readily approached and asked him if he was lost. He responded: "My mommy is lost and I can't find her." As he reached for my hand (with seemingly no fear), I looked about to see if there was a frantic mother somewhere searching for her missing child, but no one meeting that description appeared. I led him to the Customer Service counter and asked that a message with the little tike's description be voiced over their P.A. system. The mother eventually responded to the call, claimed her little boy, then immediately went back to gaming – or whatever she had been doing – on her phone. Other shoppers who had been following this episode and I just made eye-contact with corresponding glances that seemed to say "What is she doing?" About 5 minutes later, I noticed that a "grandmotherly-type" women who was with this "mother" had put the little boy into the shopping cart and was chastising him about his behavior. Without missing a beat, the "Jesus" in me said to her "Ma'am, please don't discipline him severely—he was looking for you."

Wow! What an experience that was. That little boy had looked at me and taken my hand without question —Can the world see Jesus in you? As this Scripture from the Apostle Paul's letter to Titus says, we (the people of God) must be ready and able first responders when we are "called" into all of life's situations. We must be ready to "meet necessary demands whenever the occasion may require."

As a special note to the mothers (and fathers) who may be reading this, I ask, "Are your children looking for you while you're lost in your iPhones, tablets, and other social media sites?"

Let's hope not.

—Phyllis Andrews

Run the Race Upward

"...let us lay aside every weight, and the sin which
doth so easily beset us, and let us run with patience the
race that is set before us." (Hebrews 12:1 KJV)

We live in a society that is used to doing whatever feels good right now. But instant gratification rarely brings lasting satisfaction. The Apostle Paul taught in 1 Corinthians 9:24KJV: "Do you not know that in a race that all runners compete, but only one receives the prize? So run your race that you lay hold of the prize and make it yours." Stay focused on the goal. God will give you the grace to continue to move towards it.

Now in order to run your race, you need to get fit and stay fit. "Every athlete who goes unto training conducts himself temperately and restricts himself in all things" (1 Corinthians 9:25 KJV) [emphasis "mine"]. That word "all" is a difficult concept for us to grasp. We need to live a disciplined life, physically, spiritually, and emotionally, if we want to enjoy God's plan for us. The fruit of the Spirit is self-control, and the fruit of the flesh is no control.

Paul said, "I buffet my body, handle it roughly, discipline it by hardships and subdue it, for fear that after proclaiming to others the Gospel and things pertaining to it, I myself should become unfit, not stand the test, be unapproved and rejected as a counterfeit" (1 Corinthians 9:27 KJV). So that brings us to being a "doer" of the Word. In reading His Word every day, I have found three principles to be life-changing when followed faithfully:

- Eliminate excuses and avoid procrastination. Being a doer of the Word is putting your faith into action. Can you see how this helps us run the race upward? Faith without action is dead faith (see James 2:20).
- Face the truth no matter how painful it is. Truth is the only thing that will set you free (see John 8:32). God's Word is full

of truth. Start your day in the Word of God and keep running the race upward.

- Stop feeling sorry for yourself. Understand who you are in Jesus Christ. You are more capable in Him (see Philippians 4:13).

The Bible says we are to "be doers of the Word (obey the message), and not merely listeners to it" (James 1:22). In other words, we are to apply its teaching to our everyday lives. Procrastination is one of the greatest barriers to putting God's Word into action in our lives. Spending time with God will give us the power to overcome and become a doer of the Word and continue to run our race upward.

—Tancy Elliott

Singing Through the Rain

"For our light and momentary troubles are achieving for us an eternal glory that far outweighs them all. So we fix our eyes not on what is seen, but on what is unseen. For what is seen is temporary, but what is unseen is eternal." (2 Corinthians 4:17–18 NIV)

I'm singing through the rain to chase away my pain. All the dark clouds are rolling, yes rolling away. Blue skies are up above, God's Son is shining through; I'm singing, yes, singing through the rain.

Keep singing through the rain; His joy will follow you. All the colors of the rainbow are shining for you. The signs His Son is shining through the rain are red, pink, yellow, blue, purple, green, and aqua too!

Is your life full of storms with dark clouds and pain; start singing with a smile and chase all those things away. The Son will shine on you, the Holy Spirit will comfort and guide you, and you'll start singing through those dark clouds and rain.

The Son will shower you with blessings from above. His peace will surround you and melt your troubles away. God's Son will shine upon you with the colors of the rainbow red, pink, yellow, blue, purple, green, and aqua too!

The name of God's Son is Jesus, and He loves to help us sing through the rain.

—Lynne Brown

Surety

[11]"For I know the plans I have for you," declares the LORD, "plans to prosper you and not to harm you, plans to give you hope and a future. [12]Then you will call on me and come and pray to me, and I will listen to you. [13]You will seek me and find me when you seek me with all your heart." *(Jeremiah 29:11–13 NIV)*

As a teenager, I have many decisions to make: Colleges, career paths, and what to do within life. Life at this crisp age is just starting out for me.

There was a period of time I had no idea what I wanted to do in life. Then one day, I was getting ready to go to the movies with my friends and all of a sudden the word "missions" flashed across my mind. You see, I had never dreamed of being a missionary and specifically told God that that was the last thing I wanted to do, but he had a very different idea for my future.

He ignited such a love and passion in my heart for the missions field that I plan to become a missionary someday. The beautiful thing about God's plan is that he knows best. I would have no direction for my future if it weren't for God.

He is a God who loves and wants to benefit us. Sometimes his plans may seem too big for our own abilities, but our God is able and can help us through anything that comes our way.

—Kaitlin Diemer

The Devil Made Me Do It

"When tempted, no one should say, 'God is tempting
me.' For God cannot be tempted by evil, nor does he
tempt anyone; but each person is tempted when they are
dragged away by their own evil desire and enticed."
(James 1:13–14 NIV)

"The devil made me do it," was a phrase coined by the comedian. Flip Wilson, in the early 1970's as he portrayed Geraldine, a character who habitually blamed the devil for her lack of self-control or doing whatever she wanted to do.

Often, we find ourselves using that same lame excuse or worse yet, blaming others for our failure to exercise self-control. It may be as simple as eating the extra piece of dessert or as grievous as harboring malice toward another who may have intentionally or accidently offended or hurt us. It's much easier to blame others than to take responsibility for giving in to our own desires.

The dessert may be enticing or the offense heinous, but the accountability remains with us—we often fall prey to being "dragged away by [our] own evil desire and enticed." Our actions and thoughts are injurious, not only our physical and mental well-being, but more importantly to our spiritual health—our relationship with our heavenly Father.

The antidote to this insidious practice is simple. We must first recognize our own frailties and/or sins and then confess them to God, asking His help in overcoming them. Once we do that, our battle with whatever temptation or sin can be won.

I know from personal experience that it is frequently easier said than done. But remember, the Bible tells us that all things are possible with God. He is, without a doubt, the God of the impossible.

We can be victorious over anything that may prove to be a temptation to us; but, we must take the first step and recognize our weakness or sin for what it is.

Remember, the devil can't make us do anything.

—Juanita Adamson

The Fifth Commandment

"Honor your father and your mother, that your days
may be long upon the land which the LORD your
God is giving you." (Exodus 20:12 NKJV)

God's word says to honor your parents. Honor means to prize highly, to show respect, to glory, and to exalt. Accordingly, in April 2014, God called my husband, Scott, and I to move back to Sierra Vista, Arizona. Our assignment was to love on and care for my elderly parents. A few months after my husband and I arrived, my mom was admitted to the hospital and visited the ER several times thereafter. Honestly, I wanted to just drop them off at the assisted living place and visit them when it was convenient for us. How could I be the adult to my parents and make decisions for them? It's like training your brain to think opposite of what you have learned. God definitely had different plans for us. This was a tough assignment until I gave it all to God.

After a rough morning with my parents, Scott took me for a hike in Carr Canyon. As I looked up into the beautiful sky, I asked God to speak to me as I was ready to give up. All of a sudden I felt that God said, "Sonya, I sent you here to save your parent's lives!" Tears poured down my face.

At the age of three, I was diagnosed with a severe case of the croup. The doctor told my parents if they didn't move to a drier climate I would not survive. My parents not only gave me life, but they packed up a family of six and moved across the country to save my life. They loved me just like God loves me. God loves me unconditionally by seeing only my beauty that He created. God's character is to love. God's love for me has no end. He is the God of Love.

In John 15:16-17 NKJV, Jesus says, "You did not choose Me, but I chose you and appointed you that you should go and bear fruit, and that your fruit should remain, that whatever you ask for the Father in My Name He may give you. These things I command you, that you love one another."

In the circle of life we are to honor our father and mother, whether we feel that they deserve our honor or whether they even extended appropriate love to us or not—it's all about God's love.

—Sonya Andres

Dedicated to my parents, Henry and Rosalie Webster.

The Light

"Every good and perfect gift is from above, coming down from the father of the heavenly lights, does not change like the shifting shadows." (James 1:17 NIV)

The light of goodness
Shine bright on the path I walk
Light my wayward heart

The light of my heart
Shine for righteous view to all
The light of God's love

I walk in your light
I walk surrounded in love
I walk in your faith

The light of goodness
Shine bright on the path I walk
God's luminous love.

—Sue Walker ©2015

The Right Time

"The heartfelt counsel of a friend is as sweet as
perfume and incense." (Proverbs 27:9 NLT)

Who would have thought that God would bless a homemade ornament so wonderfully? A few years ago, I selected a decoration from a basket of felt hearts at a Women's Ministry Christmas Tea. Each one had a number corresponding to a name on a list. Upon discovering its owner, we were to pray for that person. Little did I suspect that the ornament I picked belonged to a woman who was to become one of my best friends!

It amazed me how rapidly we became friends since we had just met. Soon, we were exercise buddies, enjoying special lunches, sharing our dreams, hurts and frustrations, rejoicing in Jesus, and crafting together—in other words, sharing our lives. I felt as if I had known her my entire life. It was unusual since I am basically an introvert and making friends quickly is not easy for me. But God knew I was hurting deeply and needed a good friend. In three years I had lost my three best friends, my mother, my mother-in-law, and my friend of almost twenty-five years.

Some might say the ornament I chose was by chance or accident, but I believe that it was by divine direction—God's plan for me or perhaps for both of us. The time we spent together, the encouragement we shared, and the "heartfelt counsel" are precious gifts I will always fondly hold in my heart. Often, people come into our lives, leaving memories that are soon forgotten. Others enter placing indelible imprints on our hearts—my friend did just that. She will be leaving soon to begin the next chapter in her life in another city and our friendship will change—perhaps, it will continue if that's God's plan for us. But even if our friendship is only for a season, I am so thankful to God for giving me such a wonderful friend for a brief time. She may not know why we became friends, but I know. And, Jesus, well, He understood my need and took care of me. I've learned to value all my friends as priceless gifts from God. Many have entered my life at exactly the right time. Some have remained; others have gone. I miss those who have left, but know that God has moved them on—His purpose for our friendship was accomplished.

God often blesses us with a special friend for a season, but He has given us Jesus, our friend for all the seasons of our lives.

—Juanita Adamson

The Treasure Hunt

"There's more: God's Word warns us of danger and
directs us to hidden treasure." (Psalm 19:11 MSG)

As a child, my parents and their close friends would often participate in a local treasure hunt. Climbing into our car we would speed all around the countryside following ingenious clues that had been planted in various odd locations of East Sussex, England. Clues would direct us to such spots as a wishing well, "The King's Arms" pub, a signpost, chalk pits, dew ponds, the Seven Sisters (towering chalk cliffs abutting the sea), and various other unique locations. The goal was to decipher and follow the directions encoded in each clue. Those reaching the end location first received the treasure of the day. What fun we had! Fortunately for my parents and me, our friends were gifted at deciphering complex puzzles. I do not remember if we ever actually secured the prize, but these adventures with my parents and friends are some of my treasured memories.

My parents and I were not capable of deciphering the clues in those long ago treasure hunts in England, although we had helpers; my parents' intellectual friends. Similarly, we were just like unbelievers or new Christians who neither understand nor obtain revelation from the metaphorical clues in God's Word. Jesus taught in parables so those with eyes blinded or ears blocked would not understand, but when he was alone with the disciples he would explain the parables to them.

As we search through God's Word (the Bible), the Holy Spirit deciphers truth for us. We are warned from danger and directed to hidden pearls of wisdom. There are layers and layers of revelation, the strands of which are intertwined within many books written by various authors. These authors, inspired by God, wrote in different geographical locations over a period of over three thousand years. Perhaps there are an infinite number of revelations in the Bible. It is like God's own magnificent tapestry, woven with spiritual inerrancy. He promises to unravel its wisdom to those who seek them. Just like my long-ago treasure hunts we are to continue to delve into these "spiritual clues" every day until we come to the ultimate prize—eternal life with our Savior, the Lord Jesus Christ.

Let us all persevere on our spiritual quest, our spiritual treasure hunt, until we receive the eternal prize.

—Catherine Ricks Urbalejo

Uniquely Different

"I praise you because I am fearfully and wonderfully made; your works are wonderful, I know that full well." (Psalm 139:14 NIV)

"Wow! They're gorgeous," my friend exclaimed as we took pieces of tissue paper off scarves. We spent an afternoon randomly placing "bleeding" tissue paper on white silk scarves and setting the colors with a vinegar and water solution. Once dried, the paper came off revealing our handiwork. As we looked at each scarf, we were amazed at the beautiful designs made by the colors of the paper running and blending together. Although we had used the same material and technique and, occasionally, the same color combinations, each scarf was unique, one of a kind. No two scarfs were exactly the same.

After finishing our project, I began thinking of God and His premier creation—mankind. God made us with the same composition, yet each person is a matchless creation unlike any other. Recent research indicates that even identical twins are genetically different. We know that 99% of the human body is made up of six elements: oxygen, carbon, hydrogen, nitrogen, calcium, and phosphorus. Less than 0.85% is composed of: potassium, sulfur, sodium, chlorine, and magnesium. The remaining percentage is comprised of trace elements. Basically, our physical composition is the same yet we are uniquely different, "fearfully and wonderfully made." Appearance, personalities, coloring, intellect, and many other characteristics are never the same in any two individuals. The Bible tells us that God made us. He was present at our conception, at every moment of our development, and throughout our lives.

What a marvelous discovery to realize that God is always with us and we are who we are supposed to be—flaws and all. And, not only that, but God loves us in spite of everything.

We are God's special exclusive combination of elements, spirit, soul, and a whole lot of love. But, often we forget that we are distinctive and loved of God. So, even, if at times, our circumstances are difficult, we must remember when everything seems impossible, God not only cares about what is happening to us but He is there to help us through it. He has, you might say, a vested interest in us.

Keep in mind that you are one of his works and His "works are wonderful!"

—Juanita Adamson

Veils

"...And, behold, the veil of the temple was rent in twain from the top to the bottom; and the earth did quake, and the rocks rent." (Matthew 27:51 KJV)

One of the most transcendental moments of life is the vision of a glowing bride gliding down the aisle on the arm of her father. A shimmering, ethereal vision of pure white, her face is obscured by a translucent cloud of white fluttering veil. I do not know about you, but I see the veil floating about her head as symbolizing the separation of the bride and groom. They are two unique individuals prior to marriage. The lifting of the veil upon completion of the marriage ceremony represents the union of two people, man and women becoming one flesh. No one who God has joined together should be parted. In the tabernacle of the Old Testament the veil separated the Holy of Holies where God was present from the exterior which man inhabited. It represented the separation of a Holy God from sinful man. Only once a year after a blood sacrifice of an unblemished animal could the High Priest enter the Holy of Holies. This was an annual requirement under the Mosaic Law for the removal of sin. It was also a foreshadowing of Jesus' crucifixion for the remission of all sin for all time.

Jesus was crucified, died, was buried, and three days later he rose from the dead. He was the perfect, sinless, unblemished Lamb of God. At the same time Christ died for our sins the heavy veil in the temple at Jerusalem was ripped in two-top to bottom. This veil was a replica of the veil of the Old Testament tabernacle. It was made of fine linen, blue, red and purple yarn and measured sixty feet in height thirty feet in width and was four inches thick. Ripping of such a heavy and thick veil top to bottom could not have been by a human hand. No man could have torn such a veil top to bottom and managed to do it at the exact time Christ died. The ripping of the tabernacle veil represented Christ's flesh being torn for us on the cross as He bore the sins of all mankind. It also represented that the way was opened to the Holy of Holies where

God was present. How so? Christ opened the way to God once and for all, for those who trust Jesus Christ as their Lord and Savior. No longer is there an annual requirement of animal sacrifice for remission of sins. We have direct access to God through Christ!

Once upon a time my eyes were veiled. Satan had blinded me to the truth of God's Word. Sadly, such is the lot of all unbelievers. But oh what joy! He has removed the veil from my eyes and now I see!

Are your eyes veiled or unveiled? Ask God with a pure heart to reveal Himself to you —

You will not be disappointed.

—Catherine Ricks Urbalejo

Words

Words have power
Words encourage like the wise words of a friend in a time of anguish
Words motivate like praise for a job well done
Words bring joy like good news from afar
Words calm like the gentle patter of a spring rain on a tin roof
Words cause the spirit to soar like an eagle in a thermal
Words pierce the heart like poisoned arrows shot from an adversary's bow
Words cause a sinking feeling like a physical punch to the stomach
Words beat you down like the battering ram on a castle wall
Words annoy like the buzzing of an irritating fly on a hot summer's day.

Catherine Ricks Urbalejo ©2015

There is no doubt that words have both positive and negative power. Science has verified that verbal words have energy. Sound, by which words are transmitted orally, is transmitted as kinetic energy and requires the vibration of atoms for its transmission. It cannot occur in a vacuum.

Jews in the first century believed that words were alive, active, and possessed energy. Words are the outward expression of an inward thought. The Greeks in the same period were fascinated by the amazing order in the world—the consistency of the rise of the sun and the moon, day and night, the orderly repetition of the seasons, spring, summer, fall, and winter year by year. They theorized that this order must require that a higher power or mind exist—a Creator.

Around 100 AD, the Apostle John embarked on writing the fourth and last spiritually-based gospel.[11] Unlike the earlier time in which the first three gospels were written there were now far more Greek Christians than Jewish Christians; in a ratio of about 100,000 to one. So John was faced with an interesting problem. He needed a strategy that would resonate with both Jews and Greeks. His God-inspired solution was brilliant. He employed the term "LOGOS" translated "WORD" to describe the mind of God that took on flesh in human form as Christ Jesus—a concept understandable by both the Greeks and Jews of the time.

I think the most powerful word ever used might just be "Logos" or "Word"—do you agree?

—Catherine Ricks Urbalejo

---

[11] Barclay, William. The Gospel of John. The New Daily Study Bible. WJK Press 2001

CONTRIBUTING AUTHORS

The Contributing Authors were officially invited to participate in this project by the Women of Grace Writers, based on their proficient writing skills and also on their spirit for the work of encouragement to others. Their input is greatly appreciated.

Please note that their writings are also protected under the general copyright for this publication.

Cathy Avila has been a Christian for 15 years, coming to faith in her late forties. She was recently widowed and had been married to her husband, John, for 43 years. They have a son Bryan, 36, and a daughter Annmarie, 32. Bryan and his wife, Tara, have made Cathy the grandmother of two beautiful granddaughters; Clementine who is now 4, and Penelope who is 1. After graduating from USC in 1973, she worked in Long Beach, California, for 34 years with Dr. Faris, Jr., who was a man of faith. She gave up her career 10 years ago to care for her mother who had Alzheimer's. They eventually moved to Arizona in 2005 to be near her brother in Hereford, Arizona.

Jaie Benson is an aspiring writer and entrepreneur who loves God and puts Him first in everything she does. She intends to spend the majority of the remainder of her life writing material to help others live a more God-Centered life.

Sharon Byrd is forty-seven years old and gave her life to Jesus in 2003. He delivered her from a life of homosexuality and drugs. Since then she has used her gift of writing to glorify God and minister to others. To view more of her writings visit: http://sharonbyrdcards.com/

Kaitlin Diemer is a teenage girl from Sierra Vista, Arizona. She graduated from Buena High School in 2014 and now attends Cochise College. She is working toward an Associate of Arts Degree. She plans to further her studies at the University of New Mexico in 2016 and complete a degree in Psychology.

Jerry Hatfield has written Bible lessons for church classes he has taught since his teen years. He is in his sixth year of teaching the Bible and God's love to prisoners in the Cochise County, Arizona, jail. Jerry now sends these lessons to prisoners who have gone on to serve their sentences.

Ana J. Lucore, under the Lord Jesus, is founder and executive director of *All The King's Horses Children's Ranch* in Benson, AZ. This 501(c)(3) non-profit is an Arizona-State licensed Residential Care Facility for children ages 3 – 18. To become acquainted with this miraculous work, please visit their website: http://www.atkhchildrensranch.org

Mae Mattingly, originally from Kentucky now lives in Acworth, Georgia, with Jim, her husband of 60 years. Mae's passion is sharing Christ. She has two grown children, Joy and Jill, and two grandchildren, and welcomed her first great-grandchild in April 2015.

James Moore is an ordained minister and evangelist for the Assemblies of God churches and is a leader in the areas of church revival and evangelism. His desire is to help Christians find the heart of God and then equip them to win the lost back through Christ. He is the author of *The Light Switch,* a book on personal evangelism, and has been married to his wife, Melissa, for seventeen years. James and Melissa live in southern Arizona with their two daughters, Elise and Avonlea.

David Smith is a writer and poet whose other publications can be found here: http://goo.gl/xg3g9T. He is a lifelong teacher and student of God's word. Recently relocated to Portland, Maine, David still thinks of the wonderful Huachuca Mountains whenever he reads or prays Psalm 121.

David Walker grew up in Cochise County, living in Naco, Bisbee, Fort Huachuca, Sierra Vista, and Tucson, Arizona. He attended college at

Arizona State College in Flagstaff. He served four years in the USN during Vietnam, stationed in Phoenix, and he retired to the family ranch after being a director at Life Care and Prestige nursing care facilities.

<u>Millie Wasden</u> grew up in Southern California and has lived in Sierra Vista for the last 17 years. Millie used to be very shy and insecure but never gave up the hope of overcoming this problem. Finding Christ in her life was the answer. As she started to serve God, He used her work and service to change her. In California Millie worked as a dental assistant, as a waitress in a Deli and was the proud mother of two children. She served in the PTA and for twenty years as Hospitality Chairman for her church. She has also been a Princess House Life Style Consultant in Sierra Vista for 17 years. She loves to entertain and encourage others in her life as to what God can do.

BIOGRAPHIES
WOMEN OF GRACE WRITERS

Juanita Adamson is retired from Federal service. She has been involved in children's ministries for over 20 years, teaching Sunday School, Little Kidz church, and Missionettes. She has written and directed several dramas including the yearly Christmas presentation of "Walk Thru Bethlehem." She is a Court Appointed Advocate (CASA) volunteer and enjoys crafts, writing and directing dramas, music, reading, and the outdoor adventures.

Sonya Andres recently retired from Public School Systems. She is married to her soul mate, Scott. She has been involved in many different ministries yet God gave her a twist. Being a first time author has been so rewarding to her. Her favorite word is HOPE! Jeremiah 29:11; God is HOPE.

Phyllis Andrews retired in 1995 from the Federal Government in Washington, DC, after 30 years of service and before moving to Arizona. She has been privileged to serve the Church for many years through various music and teaching ministries. Her passions include her work as the coordinator of the care center ministry, as a hospice volunteer, and as coordinator for the Women of Grace Writers. She has also participated with her husband in jail and prison ministries.

Lynne Peninger Brown was born in Oklahoma in 1947. She has twin daughters born in Japan in 1968 and a son born in the Catskill Mountains of New York in 1982. She started to sing with her God-given voice at age 11, which started her career. She was a testimony wherever she moved from a child to an adult. She eventually sang on the radio from the First Assembly of God church in Hobbs, New Mexico. She sang on TV in the Albany, NY, area, Nashville, TN, Missouri and in Arizona at Mountain View Assembly of God.

Tancy Elliott is the wife of a former pastor, and has been involved in church ministry all her life. She was one of the first Missionettes to reach the *Stairway to the Stars*. Having been active in Missionettes, youth and Sunday School ministry, kid's church plus many other activities of the church, she gives her glory to God. Among other activities of enjoyment are her love of crafts, painting, pen and ink drawings, music; she has a great love for people and a desire to help them draw closer to the Lord through her ministry.

Jane Hatfield has been writing since childhood. She continued working in the legal writing field, editing books and writing newspaper columns. Her greatest love is her Savior, Jesus Christ, and the inspiration He gives her to share through writing. Her favorite forms are devotions and journaling.

Catherine Ricks Urbalejo came to the United States in 1970 from England and has lived in Michigan, Pennsylvania, and North Carolina, before recently "retiring-rewiring" in Arizona. Her passions include her faith, family, theological research; grant writing for medicine and agriculture, particularly in cutting edge technologies, personal exercise, skiing, horses, piano, and RVing.

Cathi Rumbaugh was born in Texas in the years of the "baby boomers." She is the oldest of five children and grew up in a very strict Catholic family. Because Cathi is disabled and retired, she volunteers her time in various ministries as God calls her. She loves the Lord and promised at her baptism in 2003 to walk as a disciple of Jesus Christ. She also enjoys opportunities to fellowship with her church family and showing God's love to those who don't have a relationship with Jesus Christ nor know His forgiveness.

Sue Walker was born in Tokyo, Japan, just before the Korean War broke out. She is a wife, mother, sister, and grandmother. She started writing as a child. Poetry is her favorite. Along with writing, she enjoys cooking, crafts, and photography. She attends a Bible-based non-denominational church.

Kristen Welch earned a doctorate in Rhetoric, Composition, and the Teaching of English in 2007 and is an English Instructor for Cochise College. She is the author of *"Women with the Good News": The Rhetorical Heritage of Pentecostal Holiness Women Preachers* (CPT, 2010), *Deep Roots: Defining the Sacred Through the Voices of Pentecostal Women Preachers* (CS, 2013), and *The Role of Female Seminaries on the Road to Social Justice for Women* (with Abe Ruelas) (Wipf and Stock, 2015).

"Let the words of my mouth and the meditation of my heart
Be acceptable in Your sight, O LORD, my strength
and my Redeemer." (Psalm 19:14 NKJV)

To purchase Paperback or E-Book copies please contact:
Westbow Press
A Division of Thomas Nelson & Zondervan
http://www.bookstore.westbowpress.com/ Phone: 866-928-1240

<u>**SPECIAL NOTE**</u>: *All proceeds from the sale of this book are solely for the benefit of the not-for-profit work of the Women of Grace Ministry, Mountain View Assembly of God Church.*

~ ~ ~ ~ ~

For information on the Women of Grace Writers, please contact:
Mountain View Assembly of God
102 N. Colombo Ave., Sierra Vista, AZ 85635
Phone: 520-458-0487 mailto:mtviewag@yahoo.com
